BOOK C
READING FOR CONCEPTS

"Change is constant."   Benjamin Disraeli

BOOK C
READING

FOR CONCEPTS

Third Edition

Phoenix Learning Resources
New York

Reading for Concepts
Third Edition
Book C

Contributing Authors for the Reading for Concepts Series
Linda Barton, feature writer for *St. Louis Today*
Roberta H. Berry, elementary school teacher, writer
Barbara Broeking, journalist and educational publications editor
Eth Clifford, author of many volumes of fiction and poetry for youth
Ellen Dolan, juvenile book author
Betsy Feist, juvenile book author and reading specialist
Barbara R. Frey, Professor of Education, State University College, Buffalo, N.Y.
Ruth Harley, author and editor of young people's periodicals
Phyllis W. Kirk, children's book editor
Richard Kirk, author of science, social studies, and reading books for youth
Thomas D. Mantel, attorney and juvenile author
Marilyn F. Peachin, journalist and editor
James N. Rogers, author-editor of science and social studies resource books
James J. Pflaum, author and editor of current events periodicals
Gloria S. Rosenzweig, writer of children's books
Jean Shirley, author of juvenile books
Rosemary Winebrenner, editor of children's books
Jean White, journalist and writer of young people's reference materials

Vocabulary
Cynthia Merman, Reading and Language specialist

Project Management and Production
Kane Publishing Services, Inc.

Cover Design
Pencil Point Studios

Text Design
Jim Darby

Illustrators
Phyllis Pollema-Cahill; James Cummings; Tony Giamis, GAI

Cover Photograph
Johnny Sundby/Dakota Skies Photography

ISBN 0–7915–2105–2
3 4 5 6 7 8 9 0 05 04 03 02

TABLE OF CONTENTS

TO THE TEACHER

Purpose

This book is one of eight in the series "Reading for Concepts." It was designed to provide an opportunity for young readers to grow in reading experience while exploring a wide variety of ideas contained in the major academic disciplines.

Three basic underlying concepts are reflected in this book. They are: *Changes grow out of needs; Environment affects all living things;* and *People use the resources at hand.* The overriding concept in this book is the reason for change. To illustrate these concepts, stories have been written around intriguing pieces of information that reflect these ideas. Content has been drawn from disciplines of art, history, biology, economics, ecology, Earth science, anthropology, mathematics, space, and geography. In this way, a wide array of content for meeting various interests has been assured.

A narrative follows stories 24, 48, and 72. The narratives, largely drawn from folk literature, will provide a change of pace and are "just for fun" types of stories.

Teaching Procedure

Detailed suggestions for presenting the selections in this book will be found on pages 15 and 16 in the Teacher's Guide. Difficult words, with grade-level definitions, are listed by story on pages 6-12. Important content-area proper nouns not defined in the text are included in this listing.

Following each article is a test, which is especially designed to improve specific skills in reading. The test items were created to incorporate the thinking skills reflected in Benjamin S. Bloom's *Taxonomy of Educational Objectives*, which is explained on pages 6-7 in the Teacher's Guide.

Concept Recapitulations

After students have completed each of the three sections of this book, you may conduct a discussion to tie together the information carried in the individual articles in terms of the overall concept. Guiding questions are found on page 13 for Concept I, on page 65 for Concept II, and on page 117 for Concept III.

Have a few priming possibilities ready to suggest, or shape them out of earlier offerings from the group. Sophisticated statements and a review of specifics are not to be expected. Look for signs of mental play and the movement of information from one setting to another. It is perfectly reasonable to conclude with unanswered questions for students to ponder in retrospect. However, it is important to give students the satisfaction of enthusiastic acceptance of their early attempts at this type of open-ended speculation.

STEPS FOR THE READER

A. Turn to page 14. Look at the picture. Read the title. Think about what the story will say.

B. Study the words for this page on the list beginning on page 6.

C. Read the story carefully.

D. Put your name and the title of the story on a sheet of paper.

Number from one to eight. Begin the test on the page next to the story.

1. This question asks you to remember something the story has told you. Which of the four choices is correct for this sentence? Choose that statement.

2. The question asks you to find the word in the story that means the same as the words in slanting type. When the question gives you a paragraph or sentence number, read that part again to be sure you have the right word.

3. This question asks you to find a word that is pointed out by a smaller word. Words like *he, they,* and *it* stand for words that have been written before. Read Question 3. Who pushed further and further west? Who needed more land? The *settlers.* You can see that *they* means *settlers.* Think about your answer. In some tests like the first one, the question contains all of the words you will need. Sometimes, you will have to reread the paragraph to find the word.

4. This question wants you to think about the story. The answer is not in your book. Read the choices. Choose the sentence that is the very best guess you might make from the ideas you have just read in the story.

5. This question requires much care. You must match the test sentence *word for word* with the one in the story. Does your choice begin like the one in the story? Are all the words in the same place?

6. This question asks you to choose a statement about the entire story. Don't select an idea that fits only one small part. Your answer should fit all of the story.

7. The question points out the place in your story where you will find the right word. You must find a word that is the opposite of the one in Question 7. Think about the meaning. For the first story, look at the first paragraph. Read the first sentence again. Write the word that is the opposite of *quickly*.

8. This question wants you to think about the story. The answer is not in your book. Read the choices. Choose the sentence that is the very best guess you might make from the ideas you have read in the story.

E. Check your work. The answers for the first test are given below. Your teacher may let you use the answer key for other tests.

F. Put the number correct at the top of your paper. Now go back and recheck the answers that were wrong. Do you see now how the correct answer was better? How can you get ready to do the next test better?

G. Turn to page 170. The directions tell you how to put your score onto a record chart. Your teacher will tell you if you may write in the book. If not, he or she will help you make a copy for your notebook.

Looking for the Big Idea

See page 13 for big ideas to think about as you read.

Just for Fun

Your book has three longer stories that are just for fun. These stories, beginning on pages 62, 114, and 166, are from old folktales. There are no questions to answer.

Answers for Practice Test, page 15			
1. c	2. reservation	3. settlers	4. b
5. a	6. b	7. slowly	8. c

Vocabulary Words and Definitions

PAGE 14

forced made to do something you don't want to do
freely able to do just as you wish
further more and more
reservations a place where Native Americans live together
roamed walked around
settlers people who move to a new place

PAGE 16

explorer someone who travels to new places
native the first people to live in a place
slaves people forced to do work for no pay
somehow one way or another
tribe a group of people who are related or who live together

PAGE 18

grazing eating grass
Kenya (keˊnyə) country in east Africa
Kikuyu (ke küˊyü) a group of native people of Kenya
Maasai (māˉ sīˊ) a group of native people of Kenya
nomadic moving from place to place; not having a home
tribal in an African style
wealthy very rich

PAGE 20

alfalfa a plant grown for animals to eat
bred raised (past tense of *breed*)
honeybees insects that make honey
pollen dust in plants that helps new plants grow
scientist someone who studies animals and other things

PAGE 22

diets the foods people eat
healthy good for your body
polluted dirty and full of germs
shellfish fish that have hard coverings, such as shrimp, snails, and crabs
wild living in nature

PAGE 24

affect change
chain many things attached to each other
creatures animals

PAGE 24 continued

flashlight small lamp that you can carry; it is run by batteries
microscope machine that makes small things look bigger
snails small shellfish
sponges animals that live in the ocean
sprays poisons mixed with water to kill animals and germs
tube worms long worms that live in the ocean
wildlife animals that live outdoors

PAGE 26

chemicals natural and man-made things, like sugar, salt, air, water poisons; everything is made of chemicals
explosives strong chemicals that use force to break things into pieces
hired paid to do work
radar a way to know where airplanes and other things are in the sky

PAGE 28

ancient very many years ago
buried hidden under the ground
depend trust or believe in
fork a place where something goes in two different directions
minerals things under ground, such as coal and oil
rod a long stick
treasure something valuable or worth a lot of money

PAGE 30

billion a million million; 1,000,000,000
electricity power to give us light and make machines work
government people who make the laws
modern new
nation a country
paved covered with stones or cement
population how many people live in a place

PAGE 32

parachute a box attached to a big umbrella that can carry things from up in the air to the ground
tadpoles baby frogs
taken moved

PAGE 34

rice a white, flaky food, important to people in Asia
stairways steps that go up and down

PAGE 36

attacked struck at, or run at, tried to kill
citrus (si´trəs) fruits such as oranges, grapefruits, lemons, and limes
insects bugs; small animals with six legs
rangers people who work outdoors to keep plants and animals healthy
rid remove; kill or make go away
shipments large numbers of

PAGE 38

artificial made by people
crops vegetables grown by farmers
deal a lot of; very much
dirty not clean; full of germs
factories large buildings where people make things
reused used more than once; not thrown away

PAGE 40

energy power to make electricity and run machines
gravity the pull from the center of Earth that keeps everything together
leaked came out of a hole
material cloth
oil black liquid that is a source of energy
plastic a lightweight material that can be made into different shapes and colors

PAGE 42

barge a kind of boat used to carry things
business stores and other places that do work to earn money
Clinton, De Witt Senator and Governor of New York who was in charge of building the Erie Canal
ditch a long, narrow hole in the ground that water runs through
highway a place for traffic
passengers people who ride in boats, airplanes, and cars
states parts of a country; New York, Texas, and California are states
waterway a river that boats use

PAGE 44

interpreter someone who speaks more than one language
languages words used by people in different countries
Paiute (pī yüt´) Native American tribe in the midwestern United States
posts places where soldiers live
prisoner someone who is put in jail
rescue to free from a place
scout someone who looks around a place
supplies things you need to live
taken arrested; forced to go somewhere
treated handled

PAGE 46

harsh very cold, wet, and difficult
log wood used to build houses
scarce not a lot of something
sod dirt; earth
region place or area

PAGE 48

Aztec Indians who lived in Mexico hundreds of years ago
capital the most important city
drained removed the water from
eagle a large bird
legends stories
swampy very wet land
towers tall buildings

PAGE 50

destroyed ruined; crushed
nobles kings, queens, princes, and princesses
paid gave money
peasant poor farmer
taxes money people pay to the government or rulers
themselves those people

PAGE 52

boiling making very, very hot
followers people who agree with someone's ideas
force making people do what they don't want to do
gentle kind and friendly
peaceful not liking war
soul person

PAGE 54

cruel very mean

PAGE 54 continued
greedy wanting too many things
judged ruled
Magna Carta "Great Charter"; an important list of rules written long ago in England
power things someone is allowed to do; being strong
rebelled fought against; didn't agree with
suffered were unhappy; had a hard life

PAGE 56
coating material on the outside of something
degree how hot or cold something is
developed made; invented
distant far-away
gust big wind
launch pads what rockets sit on before they blast off
NASA National Aeronautics and Space Administration; people in charge of rockets and spaceships

PAGE 58
fuel liquid that makes planes and cars run
gasoline liquid that makes cars run; a kind of fuel
oxygen a gas that is part of air
shoots moves very quickly

PAGE 60
bored with nothing interesting or fun to do
delicious tasting very good
diner a place where people eat; restaurant
fancy full of different, beautiful things
flight a trip in the air or in outer space
float to fly without gravity
John Glenn a famous astronaut
Mercury the name of a spaceship
removed taken out of
space capsule spaceship

PAGES 62–64
bucket wooden bowl with a handle to carry water
fetch to find and bring back
lean bend at the waist
nightcap a hat people used to wear in bed
pitcher large cup to hold water
slippers shoes worn around the house
thirsty wanting something to drink

PAGE 66
avoid be safe from

PAGE 66 continued
disease sickness; chicken pox and the flu are diseases
mucus a liquid in some parts of the body
saliva a liquid in the mouth
vaccine medicine that keeps diseases away
virus (vī´rəs) germs that cause diseases

PAGE 68
Arctic the very cold area near the North Pole
coils metal circles
constructed built
engineers people who build things

PAGE 70
canoes small boats moved with a paddle
flax a kind of cloth made from plants
known called; named
pleasant sunny and not too hot or too cold; nice
strangers people you don't know

PAGE 72
adapted changed what you do so that you can live somewhere new
fringe feathers hanging down
stilts long wooden legs to stand on
wades walks into water

PAGE 74
antelope an animal like a deer
cloudy not sunny
itself all alone
stripes different-colored lines

PAGE 76
barrel big pail
desert a place that is hot and dry with little rain
stem the part of a plant that is above the ground
storage keeping or holding for a long time
tank a container to hold things, such as water

PAGE 78
area a place
geologists people who study rocks
hammer a tool for hitting nails and other things
history what happened in the past
motto a sentence that describes what you do or what you believe in

PAGE 80
clues little bits of information

PAGE 80 continued
dinosaur a large lizard that lived long ago
expert someone who knows a lot about something
famous well-known
fossils bones and other pieces of animals that died many years ago
limestone a soft stone that sometimes has fossils in it
lizard an animal that can live in the water and on land; dinosaurs were lizards
lowlands flat lands that are not high up in the mountains
millions very many; more than 1,000,000
skeleton bones of an animal

PAGE 82
concrete a kind of stone
flooded filled with water
skyscraper a very tall building
steel a strong metal used in buildings
surface the top layer; outside
weak soft; not strong

PAGE 84
snowshoes big shoes that make it easy to walk through snow
tundra part of Earth very far north where the land is always frozen

PAGE 86
dripping water falling slowly to the ground
overhead above your head; taller than you are
parrots big birds with colored feathers

PAGE 88
damage hurt
drain take away the water
Everglades a big swamp in Florida
household inside the home
erosion soil being washed away by rain
restoration making something the way it used to be

PAGE 90
egg-hatching baby chicks ready to be born and breaking out of their shells
incubator a machine that keeps eggs and babies warm
machine something with moving parts that helps people do things
orders what you are supposed to do

PAGE 90 continued
peck to make a hole with a bird's beak

PAGE 92
belongings the things you own
climate how hot or cold and wet or dry a place is
droughts (drowts) long times when there is no rain and farmers can't grow crops
dust dry dirt
periods times
search look for
soil dirt; earth

PAGE 94
air-conditioned with cold air blown in
anesthetics medicines that stop pain during an operation
exploded blew up
humidity water in the air
operating rooms places in a hospital where doctors work on sick people
temperature how hot or cold it is

PAGE 96
halfway in the middle of
harvesting picking vegetables
prairie a flat part of the country that is good for farming
wheat a grain that bread, cereal, and other foods are made from

PAGE 98
apart not near; a big distance away
depends happens because of
grown planted; raised
orchards places where fruit is grown

PAGE 100
dairy giving milk
gallons amounts that equal four quarts or sixteen cups
plenty a lot of
southern the south part of
tons amounts equal to 2,000 pounds

PAGE 102
battles fights
deerskin skin of deer used for clothing
designs pictures
hides the skins of animals

PAGE 102 continued
raised higher
scraping tool a tool made of stone that is used to clean animal hides
tanning cleaning hides so they can be made into clothes
tepees Native American homes made of animal skins

PAGE 104
crossbar something that goes across, not up and down
happenings important events
Inca Indians who lived in South America hundreds of years ago
knots bumps tied in string
meant showed
poems stories that rhyme

PAGE 106
agave a kind of plant used to make paper and rope
alphabet letters that make up words
century one hundred years
drew made pictures
folded bent over
printing writing words
scrolls long pieces of paper that are rolled up
wrote printed words and stories

PAGE 108
facts things that are true
planet round object in the sky; Earth, Mars, and Pluto are planets
temperature how cold or hot something is
volcanic came from a fiery mountain or volcano
voyage long trip

PAGE 110
carbon something needed by plants and animals to live
earthlike people like us who live on planet Earth
material a part of something
telescope a tool that makes things far away look closer
Viking probes (vī´king prōbz) spaceships sent to Mars to see what the planet is made of
zero none

PAGE 112
air pressure the force of air on something
environment all the parts of something

PAGE 112 continued
Hubble space telescope the telescope in outer space that is sending pictures back to Earth
spacecraft spaceships and rockets that explore outer space
tubes hollow containers, like drinking straws, that water runs through

PAGES 114–116
gentleman a man with good manners
gnaw to chew on
graceful pretty
handsome good-looking
honor a very nice thing; respect
marry to become someone's husband or wife
nibble to take little bites
perfect very best
powerful very strong
silky smooth and shiny
silvery-gray shiny gray color
slender thin
splendid wonderful
whiskers hairs on the face

PAGE 118
ancestors people who lived before us
ground-up mashed into tiny pieces
potters people who make bowls and plates out of clay
pottery bowls, plates, and other things made out of clay

PAGE 120
artist someone who makes pictures or sculpture
carved made things out of stone
ceremonies things done at a special time; a wedding is a kind of ceremony, and so is a birthday party
dug cut out of the ground
holy special to God
quarry a place to dig out stones (*quarries* is the plural of *quarry*)
Sioux (sü) Indians from the southeast United States
smooth without any lumps or bumps

PAGE 122
fern a kind of green plant with big leaves
ivory long teeth from animals like walruses and elephants
tusks very long teeth that grow straight out beside an animal's mouth

PAGE 122 continued

sugar cane the sugar plant, which grows on tall stems

walruses animals like seals that live in the ocean

yucca (yə′kə) plants with long, thin leaves

PAGE 124

drugstore a store that sells medicine and other things to keep you healthy

medicine something you take when you are sick that cures diseases

value full of things that are good for you

PAGE 126

cure to kill germs; to make a sick person all better

damp wet

fungus (fəng′gəs) a kind of plant that isn't green

fuzzy a soft covering that feels like fur

growth something that grows on the outside of something else

mold blue-colored growth on food that is rotten

penicillin a kind of medicine that kills germs

sour not sweet

unlike not the same as; the opposite of

wounds cuts on the body

PAGE 128

acid a liquid that can eat through rocks

cereals breakfast foods made out of corn, rice, and other grains

fungi (fən′jī) plants that are not green (plural of *fungus*)

perfume a liquid women put on their skin that smells like flowers

reindeer deer that live where it is cold and snowy

PAGE 130

diamonds stones used for jewelry that are very valuable

worn made smaller

PAGE 132

arrowheads sharp pieces of stone shaped like a triangle

curved rounded; not in a straight line

jewelry rings, earrings, necklaces

knives sharp tools for cutting

lava fiery rocks that come out of volcanoes

Mayan (mī′ən) Native Americans who lived in Mexico hundreds of years ago

PAGE 132 continued

mirror something very shiny that you can see yourself in

ornaments pretty things

spears long sticks with a point at the end

Yellowstone National Park a very big park in Wyoming, Idaho, and Montana

PAGE 134

crystals pieces of stone that you can see through

rate amount of time

quartz a kind of rock

synthetic made by people; not found in nature

vibrating moving very quickly

PAGE 136

bloom grow leaves and flowers

cornfield a place where corn is grown

pasture grass

PAGE 138

coast the land that is next to the ocean

salmon fish that people like to eat

stretching from one place to another

waterfalls water from a river that falls from higher up

PAGE 140

bare with no plants growing

blown moved by the wind

PAGE 142

dried with the water taken out

fertilizer chemicals put on plants to help them grow

iodine a medicine that kills germs

kombu seaweed eaten by Japanese people

simple not having many different parts

PAGE 144

beaches sand near the ocean

Dead Sea a lake in the Middle East that has a lot of salt in its water

dye something that changes the color of water

Middle East a part of the world that includes Egypt, Israel, and Arabia

mined dug up from deep in the ground

pure only one thing, with nothing else mixed in

PAGE 146
close quarters living very near other people
electronic things that use electricity, such as TVs and radios
harmony happily, without fighting
high-quality very good
living quarters houses or homes; where you live
miniature tiny; very small

PAGE 148
beehives places where bees live and make honey
bricks stones used to build houses
protect keep safe

PAGE 150
bamboo a plant with stems like wood
carts big boxes with wheels that are pulled by animals; people can ride in carts

PAGE 152
breeze a soft wind
form take the shape of
palm a tree with very big leaves
shelter a safe place
slanting not straight across or up and down; higher on one side than on the other
strips long, thin pieces

PAGE 154
daring brave
linen a kind of cloth
navigators sailors
Phoenicia an old country in the Middle East
resource something important and useful
routes ways to get somewhere
tin a metal
traders people who buy and sell things

PAGE 156
cheaply for very little money
choice one way to do something
experienced educated; smart
hull the outside of a ship
masts tall poles on a ship that hold the sails
member a person who is part of a group

PAGE 158
clumsy big and hard to move
colonies places owned by other countries
since because

PAGE 160
arch half circle
Babylonians people from Babylonia, an old country in the Middle East
conquered ruled by force
duct short tube or pipe
empire land owned by a country
Romans people from Rome, the capital of Italy
structures buildings

PAGE 162
advances discoveries; new ways of doing something
complicated with many parts
grain the seeds of some cereal plants
systems ways of doing something
tally counting; adding up
technology science; inventing

PAGE 164
altitudes places high up, such as tops of mountains or outer space
breathe to take air into the lungs
helmets hard hats to protect the head
pilot the person who is in charge of a plane or spaceship
pressures air pressures; when the air outside something is stronger than the air inside
research studies; learning
rocket a plane that flies very fast in outer space
rubber a material that is easy to bend and make into different shapes

PAGES 166–169
beauty things that are pretty to look at
bet a game where you say you can do something and your friend says you can't do it
chariot a big two-wheeled cart pulled by animals that people can ride in
clever smart
collect to win; to get what is owed to you
dwarf a very short person
forgive to stop being angry at
goddess a woman god
grumbled complained; said he was unhappy
lightning flashes of light during a storm
mischief playing tricks
ninth nine times
punish to make pay a penalty
replace to give back
rumbling a loud noise

I

Changes Grow Out of Needs

In this section, you will read about changes that grow out of needs. You will read about these things in the areas of anthropology, biology, Earth science, ecology, (reactions to environment), economics, geography, history, and space.

Keep these questions in mind when you are reading.

1. What are some basic needs of people?

2. What changes can you think of that have taken place to meet these needs better?

3. Have any of these changes affected me?

4. Have these changes been good for us?

5. Have any of these changes been harmful?

Look on pages 6-8 for help with words in this section you don't understand.

The Day the Native People Cried

1   The line of Potawatomi Indians moved slowly ahead. The old people and children cried when they looked back. The Potawatomi did not want to leave their home in Indiana. Many said they would rather die than go, but they had to leave.

2   Once the forests and plains had belonged only to the Native Americans. They had roamed freely over their land. Then new settlers came to America. Things began to change. As the settlers pushed further and further west, they needed more land. The native people were forced to sell their land to the settlers and move from their homes to other land, called reservations.

3   In the 1840s, the last Native Americans in Indiana, the Miami, left Indiana for their reservation in Kansas. The Miami were not happy there. Many died that first cold winter.

4   The native people wanted to go back to the places they knew as home. But settlers lived in these places now. Each year more settlers came. The Native Americans could never return again.

1. The forests and plains had once belonged to the
   - a. animals.
   - c. Native Americans.
   - b. settlers.
   - d. birds.

2. The word in the story that means *land set aside for Native Americans to live on* is _____.

3. The story says: "As the settlers pushed further and further west, *they* needed more land." The word *they* means

   _____.

4. The story does not say this, but from what we have read, we can tell that
   - a. all of the settlers stayed in the East.
   - b. many Native Americans could not get used to their new life.
   - c. the Miami Indians left Kansas to go to New York.

5. How did the Miami Indians feel about living in Kansas? (Which sentence is exactly like the one in your book?)
   - a. The Miami were not happy there.
   - b. The Miami were very happy there.
   - c. The Miami were not a happy tribe.

6. The main idea of the whole story is that
   - a. the Native Americans liked to move to new lands.
   - b. native peoples had to leave their land when settlers came.
   - c. the Potawatomi liked to stand in lines.

7. The word in paragraph 1, sentence 1, that is the opposite of *quickly* is _____.

8. Which of the following does this story lead you to believe?
   - a. Native Americans still live together in Indiana.
   - b. The Potawatomi were glad to see the settlers come.
   - c. It is not easy to leave a home you love.

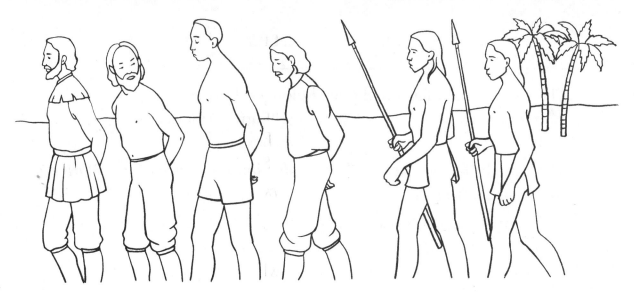

Nine Years from Home

1   Cabeza de Vaca was a Spanish explorer. In 1528, his ship was washed up on a small island near Texas. The explorers called it Bad Luck Island. Most of his group died, but somehow he and three others lived. Two of these were explorers. One was a tall black slave.

2   The men were found by a native tribe and kept by them as slaves. They all lived a hard life, often going for days without food. Sometimes they ate earth and wood!

3   After a long time, the four men escaped. They lived among friendlier tribes. They took care of the sick. In return, people gave them food and animal skins. Cabeza de Vaca came to admire these people and their life.

4   One day the explorers met some Spanish soldiers in Mexico who were capturing native people for slaves. When the soldiers went back to Spain, they took the explorers with them. After nine long years, Cabeza de Vaca finally went home.

5   Back in Spain, Cabeza de Vaca did not forget his life as a slave. He tried to stop slavery by writing about his life in the New World.

1. Cabeza de Vaca was shipwrecked on an island near
    a. Mexico.
    c. Florida.
    b. Texas.
    d. Spain.

2. The word in the story that means *a person who tries to discover new places* is _____.

3. The word *his* in paragraph 5 means _____.

4. The story does not say this, but from what we have read, we can tell that
    a. Cabeza de Vaca was looking for Bad Luck Island.
    b. Cabeza de Vaca liked Texas better than Spain.
    c. Cabeza de Vaca did not give up easily.

5. What did the explorers call the island they landed on? (Which sentence is exactly like the one in your book?)
    a. The explorers called it Cabeza de Vaca.
    b. The explorers called it Bad Luck Island.
    c. The explorers called it Texas Island.

6. The main idea of the whole story is that
    a. people sometimes must suffer hardships in order to survive.
    b. Cabeza de Vaca did not like being a slave.
    c. we can learn a great deal about early Americans by reading Cabeza de Vaca's books.

7. The word in paragraph 1, sentence 4, that is the opposite of *lived* is
    _____.

8. Which of the following does this story lead you to believe?
    a. Cabeza de Vaca had a good time in Texas.
    b. Cabeza de Vaca was glad to get home.
    c. Cabeza de Vaca always had bad luck.

Two Tribes

1   For hundreds of years, the Maasai and the Kikuyu have lived as neighbors. They live in an African nation called Kenya.

2   The Maasai move about, following their grazing herds. The wealthy Maasai are the families that have the most cattle. Because the Maasai are nomadic, it is difficult for their children to go to school. Many changes have come to Kenya now, but not to the Maasai. They like their nomadic way of life and see no reason to change it.

3   The Kikuyu are very different. They have welcomed the winds of change. Kikuyu children go to school in great numbers. They leave their tribal clothing behind. Their clothes are just like those worn by others around the world. Kikuyu men and women work in the cities where many have become doctors, lawyers, and businesspeople.

4   The world around the Kikuyu has changed. They want to be part of this new world.

1. The Maasai live in
   a. Kenya.   c. Algeria.
   b. the Congo.   d. Italy.

2. The word in the story that means *people who live near each other* is

   _____.

3. The word *they* in paragraph 4 means _____.

4. The story does not say this, but from what we have read, we can tell that
   a. all children in Africa must go to school.
   b. neighbors have to be friends in Africa.
   c. the Kikuyu will help their country grow.

5. Which Maasai are wealthy? (Which sentence is exactly like the one in your book?)
   a. Wealthy Maasai have beautiful tribal clothing.
   b. Wealthy Maasai can stay in one place.
   c. The wealthy Maasai are the families that have the most cattle.

6. The main idea of the whole story is that
   a. the Maasai ride their cattle into the big cities.
   b. the Maasai have stayed as they are but the Kikuyu have changed.
   c. Kikuyu children wear their tribal clothes to school.

7. The word in paragraph 2, sentence 2, that is the opposite of *easy* is

   _____.

8. Which of the following does this story lead you to believe?
   a. Some people choose not to change their ways.
   b. There are no schools in Kenya.
   c. Most African doctors live in Kenya.

The Fussy Bees

1 Are you a fussy eater? Do you like some foods, but not others? Bees can be fussy, too! They don't like the smell of certain flowers. They don't like flowers in which pollen is hard to reach. Bees stay away from these kinds of plants.

2 When bees fly from flower to flower, they carry the pollen which helps plants grow. Without bees, some plants might disappear, never to grow again.

3 Honeybees do not like alfalfa because the pollen is hard to reach. Alfalfa is a plant farmers grow as food for their animals. Farmers needed help to get honeybees to come to the alfalfa.

4 A scientist in the U.S. Department of Agriculture began to breed honeybees. He bred them to like alfalfa. Soon he had honeybees that liked alfalfa better than any other kind of plant! Now he is trying to breed bees that will like plants they have never liked before. Someday scientists may breed bees to go to any plant we choose for them.

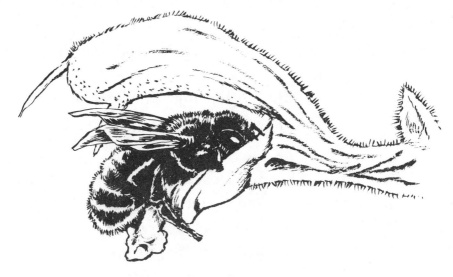

FIND THE ANSWERS

1. Honeybees did not like alfalfa because
   - a. it was too far away.
   - c. the pollen was hard to reach.
   - b. it grew too tall.
   - d. the smell was too strong.

2. The word in the story that means *a plant that is grown as food for animals* is _____ .

3. The word *he* in paragraph 4 means the _____ in the U.S. Department of Agriculture.

4. The story does not say this, but from what we have read, we can tell that
   - a. honeybees are important to many farmers.
   - b. pollen is the best food for animals to eat.
   - c. farmers grow a lot of alfalfa for their bees.

5. What is true about some bees? (Which sentence is exactly like the one in your book?)
   - a. They don't like the smell of certain flowers.
   - b. They don't like the way certain plants look.
   - c. They don't like the way certain farmers act.

6. The main idea of the whole story is that
   - a. scientists hate honeybees who eat lots of pollen.
   - b. scientists are breeding new kinds of honeybees.
   - c. scientists make bees smell better than alfalfa.

7. The word in paragraph 2, sentence 2, that is the opposite of *appear* is _____ .

8. Which of the following does this story lead you to believe?
   - a. Farmers don't want to grow any more alfalfa.
   - b. Scientists find better ways of doing things.
   - c. All scientists have become very fussy eaters.

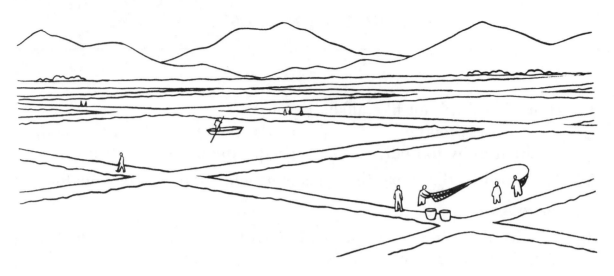

Some Very Wet Farms

1   You know that corn and wheat are grown on farms. On some farms, animals such as pigs, goats, and turkeys are raised. Many people don't know this, but very wet farms are used for raising fish and shellfish. The Chinese were the first to farm water plants and animals. They have had seafood farms for over 3,500 years!

2   People who catch seafood in the wild face many problems. In bad weather, their boats cannot go out. The fishing grounds may be empty. In recent years, water in some areas has become polluted. Eating fish from those areas is not healthy. Seafood farms solve these problems. These fish and shellfish do not live in the wild. They are fed healthy diets and live in clean water. They grow bigger, although some people do not think that they taste as good as wild fish do.

3   Today, China still has the most seafood farms. It raises over 11 million tons of seafood every year. Many other countries also raise seafood on farms. In America, we have seafood farms, too. Perhaps there is one near where you live.

FIND THE ANSWERS

1. The fish and shellfish in seafood farms are fed
    - a. healthy diets.
    - b. goats and turkeys.
    - c. water plants.
    - d. corn.

2. The word in the story that means *water plants and animals* is
    _____.

3. The word *it* in paragraph 3 means _____.

4. The story does not say this, but from what we have read, we can tell that
    - a. there are no seafood farms in the United States.
    - b. you should not eat fish caught in the wild.
    - c. the Chinese eat a lot of seafood.

5. Which country has the most seafood farms? (Which sentence is exactly like the one in your book?)
    - a. In America, almost all of our seafood comes from seafood farms.
    - b. Today, China still has the most seafood farms.
    - c. In fact, over 11 million tons of seafood comes from seafood farms every year.

6. The main idea of the whole story is that
    - a. Seafood farms solve many problems.
    - b. The Chinese were the first people to have seafood farms.
    - c. There are many different types of farms.

7. The word in paragraph 2, sentence 3, that is the opposite of *full* is
    _____.

8. Which of the following does the story lead you to believe?
    - a. Some things haven't changed much in China in the last 3,500 years.
    - b. Seaweed is sometimes grown on farms.
    - c. People eat more fish than turkey.

Life from the Sea

1   Many scientists are quiet persons. But they make big changes in our lives. These women and men have strong needs to know how things work. One important woman spent her life studying life from the sea.

2   Rachel Carson knew about many strange creatures, such as tube worms, green sponges, and tiny snails that live on seaweed.

3   Very late at night, she looked at all these creatures under her microscope. When she was through, she took a pail and a flashlight to walk to the sea. With great care, she returned all the creatures to their home.

4   To Rachel Carson, the sea was a dark world with many secrets of life. She studied the waves and tides. She knew they made changes in the lives of tiny animals that lived in the sea and on shore.

5   Rachel Carson also helped us to see that changes people make which affect tiny plant and animal life can mean changing the whole chain of life. Today we use many kinds of sprays against certain bugs and pests. But now we know that we must be careful about how these sprays change wildlife and plants.

FIND THE ANSWERS

1. Green sponges live
    a. in pails.
    b. in the sea.
    c. in the forest.
    d. on seaweed.

2. The word in the story that means *a tool to make small things look larger* is _____.

3. The word *they* in paragraph 1 takes the place of the word

   _____.

4. The story does not say this, but from what we have read, we can tell that
    a. Rachel Carson was a scientist because she was paid well.
    b. Rachel Carson was a scientist because she loved nature.
    c. Rachel Carson studied nature because she was quiet.

5. What did Rachel Carson do with the animals she studied? (Which sentence is exactly like the one in your book?)
    a. She kept the animals in a pail.
    b. With great care, she returned all the creatures to their home.
    c. She carefully put them all under the microscope.

6. The main idea of the whole story is that
    a. we can learn from people who study animals and plants.
    b. people who study animals and plants live alone.
    c. it is fun to use a microscope.

7. The word in paragraph 3, sentence 1, that is the opposite of

   early is _____.

8. Which of the following does the story lead you to believe?
    a. It's best to study plants at night.
    b. Wildlife gets along best without tiny animals.
    c. We should be more careful of the effect of poisons on animal life.

Bring on the Rain

1   In 1891, the U.S. government hired an airplane pilot to make it rain. He dropped explosives into clouds from his plane. Did the explosions bring on the rain? Or did it just happen to rain after the pilot did his work? We don't know. Today we are still looking for ways to make it rain when it has been dry for a long time. People cannot live without water. But we don't use explosives anymore. Today people can use radar, computers, and chemicals to try to make rain.

2   On the ground, a crew will study the clouds in an area by using radar and weather maps on the Internet. They send the information to an airplane pilot. The pilot flies into a cloud and drops a special chemical. This is called *seeding* the cloud. If the seeding works, the cloud grows larger. It draws in moist air. The moisture forms into drops of water, which freeze. When the ice gets heavy it falls as rain.

3   In 1996 there was a drought in the Southwest that caused great hardship. Some ranchers and farmers hired a cloud-seeding company to make it rain. That summer they had more rain than usual. Did the cloud seeding bring on the rain? We still don't know for sure.

FIND THE ANSWERS

1. In 1891 the pilot dropped explosives into clouds
   - a. by mistake.
   - b. in a balloon.
   - c. to blow them up.
   - d. to make it rain.

2. The word in the story that means a *work group* is

   _____.

3. The story says: "When the ice gets heavy it falls as rain." The word *it* means _____.

4. The story does not say this, but from what we have read, we can tell that
   - a. cloud seeds need rain to grow into clouds.
   - b. farmers and ranchers both need rain.
   - c. the U.S. government proved that cloud seeding works.

5. What happens if seeding a cloud works? (Which sentence is exactly like the one in your book?)
   - a. If the seeding works, the cloud grows larger.
   - b. If the seeding works, the cloud freezes.
   - c. If the seeding works, the seeds explode.

6. The main idea of the whole story is that
   - a. pilots seed clouds to try to control the weather.
   - b. we can never change the weather.
   - c. rain falls only when the clouds are seeded.

7. The word in paragraph 2, sentence 6, that is the opposite of *dry* is

   _____.

8. Which of the following does the story lead you to believe?
   - a. No one will ever know whether cloud seeding works.
   - b. Over the last 100 years, cloud seeding has become more scientific.
   - c. There is no point in seeding clouds because it is bound to rain sooner or later.

27

The Magic Sticks

1   A woman walks slowly across a field as a man watches. The woman is holding a divining rod in her hands. The divining rod is a stick shaped like a Y. It has been cut from the branch of a tree. The fork of the Y points up. Suddenly the woman stops. The stick is now pointing straight down. "Dig in this spot," she says. The man cries, "Water! We found water!"

2   The divining rod goes back to ancient times. With these "magic sticks," as they were called, people looked for gold and silver underground. They looked for minerals. They even tried to find buried treasure. Later, the magic sticks were used most often to find underground water. This way of looking for water is called water witching. It did not always work.

3   Our great need to find water underground has not changed. But today, we do not depend on magic. Instead, we ask the help of our scientists.

28

1. The woman with the divining rod found
   - a. water.
   - b. gas.
   - c. gold.
   - d. oil.

2. The word in the story that means *the place where something branches or divides* is _____.

3. The story says: "People looked for gold and silver underground. *They* looked for minerals." The word *they* means the

   _____.

4. The story does not say this, but from what we have read, we can tell that
   - a. the divining rod can find anything at anytime.
   - b. people will try many things in their search for water.
   - c. many water witches can be found out in the fields.

5. What is this way of looking for water called? (Which sentence is exactly like the one in your book?)
   - a. This way of looking for water is called witchcraft.
   - b. This way of looking for water is called water witching.
   - c. This way of looking for witches is called water science.

6. The main idea of the whole story is that
   - a. people once believed divining rods could find water.
   - b. most people found buried treasure in every field.
   - c. Y-shaped magic sticks always had to point down.

7. The word in paragraph 1, sentence 2, that is the opposite of *dropping* is _____.

8. Which of the following does this story lead you to believe?
   - a. Water is always easy to find.
   - b. Some people today believe in water witching.
   - c. Scientists have no better ways of finding water.

Nation of Villages

1   There are more than 650,000 villages in India. The people in the villages are farmers who farm small pieces of land. They do not live on their farms. Instead, they live in mud huts in their villages. They grow rice and other crops on their farms, and they also raise animals.

2   The village farmers are important to India. Almost a billion people live in India, and all of these people need the food the farmers grow. In the past, farmers could not grow enough crops to feed India's growing population. India had to buy rice and grain from other countries. Many people were always hungry.

3   But the old ways of farming are slowly changing. The Indian government is sending modern farming tools and teachers into the villages. The teachers help farmers use the new tools. Farmers can buy new types of seeds. With these seeds, they can grow more food.

4   India is beginning to grow most of the food it needs. Life for the villagers has gotten better. Many villages now have paved roads and electricity. And most villages have schools for the children.

FIND THE ANSWERS

1. The farmers in India live in
   - a. cities.
   - b. farmhouses.
   - c. mud huts.
   - d. log cabins.

2. The word in the story that means *the plants farmers grow* is
   _____.

3. The word *they* in paragraph 3, sentence 5, means _____.

4. The story does not say this, but from what we have read, we can tell that
   - a. children in India learn how to use farm tools at their village schools.
   - b. there are no cities in India.
   - c. in the past, the roads in most Indian villages were not paved.

5. How do the teachers help the farmers? (Which sentence is exactly like the one in your book?)
   - a. The teachers help farmers pave their roads.
   - b. The teachers have help farmers use the new tools.
   - c. The teachers have help farmers learn to read and write.

6. The main idea of the whole story is that
   - a. villagers in India lead a hard life.
   - b. the new ways of farming have made life better for everyone in India.
   - c. India needs more farmers to feed the growing population.

7. The word in paragraph 2, sentence 3, that is the opposite of *future* is
   _____.

8. Which of the following does the story lead you to believe?
   - a. The villages in India are becoming cities.
   - b. Farmers in India do not grow wheat or vegetables.
   - c. More children go to school in India now than in the past.

Beavers by Parachute

1   The beavers were building a dam in a small stream. The land around the stream was dry. Few plants grew there. Not many animals came to the stream.

2   When the dam was finished, there was a new pond. The pond made many changes in the land. The pond caught and held rainwater. Fish grew in great numbers in the pond. Frogs came and soon there were new tadpoles swimming in the water. Birds came to feed on the fish and tadpoles. Wild animals came to drink the clear water and eat the new water plants.

3   These beavers had not always lived here. They had been brought here by people who wanted to make this dry land rich again. The beavers had been taken from another stream far away and brought to this stream by airplane. The beavers, in special boxes, had been dropped by parachutes. When the boxes had hit the ground, the beavers had jumped out and run to the stream. The changing of the land had begun.

1. The land around the stream was
   - a. hot.
   - b. wet.
   - c. dry.
   - d. dirty.

2. The word in the story that means *something built across a river or stream that holds back the water* is _____ .

3. The story says: "The land around the stream was dry. Few plants grew *there*." The word *there* tells us few plants grew on the

   _____ .

4. The story does not say this, but from what we have read, we can tell that
   - a. fish eat the birds and the wild animals.
   - b. water can make a land rich in many ways.
   - c. beavers don't like water in their homes.

5. What did the pond do? (Which sentence is exactly like the one in your book?)
   - a. The pond caught and held rainwater.
   - b. The pond caught all the frogs and fish.
   - c. The pond caught the clear-water birds.

6. The main idea of the whole story is that
   - a. there are beavers living in every stream.
   - b. the dam the beavers made changed the land.
   - c. rainwater does not fall into many ponds.

7. The word in paragraph 2, sentence 1, that is the opposite of *started* is _____ .

8. Which of the following does this story lead you to believe?
   - a. Living things in an area depend on each other.
   - b. Beavers like to jump from airplanes with parachutes.
   - c. Rich people like all their land to stay dry.

Mountainside Farming

1   Suppose you are in an airplane flying over Japan. You look down and see what seem to be wide steps around the sides of mountains. The wide steps are green fields. From the air, these fields look like great green stairways.

2   Japan is a small country. All of its land would not fill California, yet it holds almost half as many people as live in the whole United States. The Japanese farmers must use every bit of their land to grow enough crops to feed the population.

3   Much of Japan is covered by mountains, so even the mountainsides must be farmed. The Japanese farmer grows rice in little fields called "paddies." These paddies are cut like stair steps down the mountainsides. Low walls of earth divide the paddies. Rice grows in the water held by these walls.

4   Turning mountains into farms was not easy. But Japanese farmers needed to do it. How else could they feed so many people?

34

1. From the air, the fields of Japan look like great green
    a. grasshoppers.   c. stairways.
    b. elephants.   d. blankets.

2. The word in the story that means *rice fields* is
    _____.

3. The word *it* in paragraph 2 means the small country of
    _____.

4. The story does not say this, but from what we have read, we can tell that
    a. the Japanese like to play checkers.
    b. the Japanese fly around too much.
    c. rice is an important food in Japan.

5. How big is Japan? (Which sentence is exactly like the one in your book?)
    a. All of its land would not fill Connecticut.
    b. All of its land would not fill California.
    c. All of its land would not fill Australia.

6. The main idea of the whole story is that
    a. Japanese farmers found a way to use more land.
    b. Japanese farmers wanted to see new faces.
    c. Japanese farmers wanted to live in California.

7. The word in paragraph 1, sentence 3, that is the opposite of *narrow* is _____.

8. Which of the following does the story lead you to believe?
    a. The Japanese have made wise use of their land.
    b. Rice paddies are very good to eat in airplanes.
    c. You can walk up wide steps around the mountains.

The Bug War

1   We use sprays to get rid of bugs. But the bugs are still with us. Now scientists are using bugs to fight bugs!

2   Insects called gypsy moths attacked our forests. Rangers sprayed the gypsy moths, but still they came in great numbers. Then scientists brought from Europe hundreds of thousands of special small flies. These flies ate the eggs of the gypsy moths. The flies helped save the forests.

3   The citrus blackfly attacked the fruit trees in Florida and California. Scientists brought beetles and wasps from Asia and Australia. The beetles and wasps were brought in by airplane in special boxes! The beetles and wasps attacked the citrus blackfly. The fruit trees were saved.

4   The United States has set up some stations where shipments of insects can come in. These shipments come from all over the world. They come from places as near as Canada, and as far away as Israel and Africa.

5   The war with bugs goes on. Using nature's own way, scientists may win this war someday.

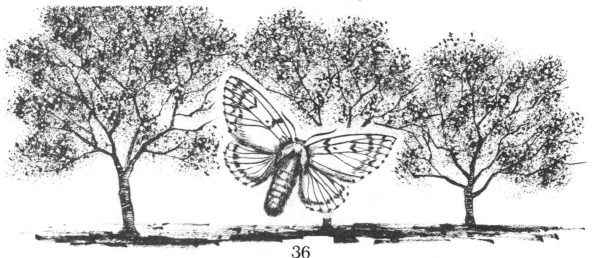

1. We use sprays to get rid of
   - a. people.
   - b. cows.
   - c. bugs.
   - d. fish.

2. The word in paragraph 1, sentence 1, that means *free from* is

   _____ .

3. The word *they* in paragraph 4, sentence 3, takes us back to the

   word _____ .

4. The story does not say this, but from what we have read, we can tell that
   - a. beetles and wasps can fly as fast as airplanes.
   - b. some insects are helpful and some are harmful.
   - c. gypsy moths keep attacking beetles and wasps.

5. What did the flies eat? (Which sentence is exactly like the one in your book?)
   - a. The flies ate the eggs of the citrus beetles.
   - b. These flies ate the eggs of the gypsy moths.
   - c. The gypsy flies ate the eggs of the wasps.

6. The main idea of the whole story is that
   - a. most bugs fight wars in Australia and in Asia.
   - b. scientists use some bugs to get rid of other bugs.
   - c. insects are getting into all our shipping stations.

7. The word in paragraph 2, sentence 5, that is the opposite of

   destroy is _____ .

8. Which of the following does this story lead you to believe?
   - a. All kinds of insects want to come here from Australia.
   - b. We might have less fruit without the help of some bugs.
   - c. There are many thousands of gypsy moths all over Europe.

The Town That Saved Its Water

1   Water costs money. In some places water is hard to get. What happens when a town has these problems? A small town in California found a happy answer.

2   Very little rain ever fell there. The town had no water of its own. The water it used was brought in from a river 300 miles away. As more people came to live in the town, more water was needed. Now water had to be brought in from 600 miles away. All this cost a great deal of money.

3   The town made a plan. It found a way to clean its "dirty" water. Once cleaned, the water was reused in many ways. Five artificial lakes were built. Here people could swim and fish and go boating. They could have picnics in their new parks. Farmers had more water for their crops. New factories can be built, now that they have the promise of enough water.

4   In most places, water is used and thrown away. The town that saved its water has saved the town!

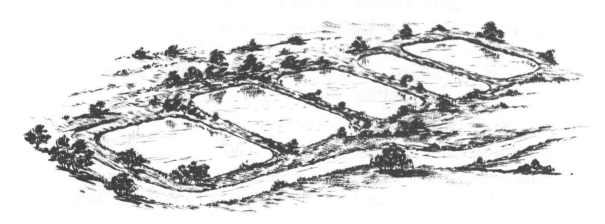

1. The town that saved its water was in
    a. Idaho.   c. New Jersey.
    b. Arizona.   d. California.

2. The word in the story that means *buildings in which things are made by machines* is _____ .

3. The story says: "The town made a plan. *It* found a way to clean its 'dirty' water." The word *it* means the _____ .

4. The story does not say this, but from what we have read, we can tell that
    a. water can be found everywhere.
    b. people cannot live without water.
    c. some crops do not need much water.

5. Why did the town in California bring water from a river 300 miles away? (Which sentence is exactly like the one in your book?)
    a. The town had no people or rivers.
    b. The town had no water of its own.
    c. The town only liked river water.

6. The main idea of the whole story is that
    a. a small town solved its water problem.
    b. water cannot be cleaned enough to reuse.
    c. water is free for people in small towns.

7. The word in paragraph 2, sentence 4, that is the opposite of *less* is _____ .

8. Which of the following does this story lead you to believe?
    a. Farmers will only use dirty water.
    b. California is not a good place to live.
    c. Good planning can help a city grow.

Looking for "Black Gold"

1   Oil is so important it is sometimes called black gold. Almost half our energy comes from oil. We use it to run our cars and factories and to heat our homes, offices, and schools. Many everyday things are made from oil. Your shirt may have oil in the material. The soap you wash it in might also made with oil. Your favorite plastic toy is made from oil.

2   Oil is hard to find, because it is trapped deep under the earth. Once the only way people knew there was oil someplace was if it leaked out of the ground. Today, however, we have many ways of finding oil. One tool measures gravity. Places where gravity is weaker are more likely to have oil. Another tool measures sound waves. Sound waves travel through different kinds of rocks at different speeds. We can use them to find the rocks that have oil in them.

3   We need a lot of oil, and we are using up the oil wells we know about. Soon we must find new ways of looking for this black gold.

FIND THE ANSWERS

1. Oil is sometimes called
   - a. black rocks.
   - b. black energy.
   - c. black gold.
   - d. black ink.

2. The word in the story that means *buildings where goods are made* is

   _____.

3. The word *it* in paragraph 1 means _____.

4. The story does not say this, but from what we have read, we can tell that
   - a. oil runs in rivers of gold.
   - b. oil is found only under water.
   - c. oil is found in rocks.

5. Why do sound waves help to find oil? (Which sentence is exactly like the one in your book?)
   - a. Sound waves travel through different kinds of rocks at different speeds.
   - b. They measure the pull of gravity on rocks that have oil in them.
   - c. Sound waves tell us where the oil has seeped out of the ground.

6. The main idea of the whole story is that
   - a. many things are made from oil.
   - b. oil is hard to find because it is trapped under the ground.
   - c. people spend a lot of time looking for oil.

7. The word in paragraph 2, sentence 1, that is the opposite of *freed* is

   _____.

8. Which of the following does the story lead you to believe?
   - a. Oil was first found by measuring gravity.
   - b. Our lives would be very different if we didn't have oil.
   - c. We will never run out of oil.

Clinton's Ditch

1   The Erie Canal was opening. That day in November 1825 was important to De Witt Clinton. Soon it was important to the whole country. Clinton had talked for years about the need for a new waterway in New York State. At first, people laughed at "Clinton's Ditch." But when the waterway was finished, cargo boats had a shortcut from the Atlantic Ocean to the Great Lakes.

2   The first boats were pulled by horses. People were surprised at how fast the boats moved—1 1/2 miles an hour! Passengers paid 1 1/2 cents a mile.

3   The Canal was used for many years. It helped New York City grow by bringing new business to the city. Other cities along the Canal grew, too. Soon other states began to build canals.

4   In the 1850s, railroads were built. Soon railroads began to take business away from the Canal.

5   Today, the Erie Canal is still being used. It is part of the New York State Barge Canal System. But it is no longer a busy water highway.

1. Clinton's Ditch was in the state of
   a. New Jersey.
   c. New York.
   b. North Carolina.
   d. New Mexico.

2. The word in the story that means *a quicker way of getting from place to place* is _____.

3. The story says: "The Canal was used for many years. *It* helped New York City grow by bringing new business to the city." The word *it* takes us back to the word _____.

4. The story does not say this, but from what we have read, we can tell that
   a. many people laughed at the horses.
   b. one man's dream helped many people.
   c. the Canal could not open in November.

5. How long was the Canal used? (Which sentence is exactly like the one in your book?)
   a. The Canal was used for a long time.
   b. The Canal was used for twenty years.
   c. The Canal was used for many years.

6. The main idea of the whole story is that
   a. canals are used for swimming and fishing.
   b. horses are only good for pulling riverboats.
   c. the Erie Canal was once an important waterway.

7. The word in paragraph 3, sentence 4, that is the opposite of *quit* is _____.

8. Which of the following does this story lead you to believe?
   a. Canals are never used these days.
   b. New ways of travel replace older ways.
   c. Transportation is not important to business.

A Brave Fighter

1   Winnemucca was the daughter of a Paiute chief. She lived in the 1800s. The Native Americans then were often tricked and treated badly by new settlers. When Native Americans were forced onto reservations, they often had trouble getting food and supplies. Sometimes they could go to the army posts for help.

2   Winnemucca was a clever woman. She spoke English, French, Spanish, and other languages. She also knew many of the languages of other tribes. She soon became a scout and an interpreter at an army post in Nevada. During that time, there was a war between the Paiutes and the fiece Bannock tribe. Winnemucca's father was taken prisoner.

3   Many Paiutes were afraid to travel into the enemy land. But Winnemucca felt she had to go. She traveled alone more than 100 miles, often going without sleep. She crossed the roughest part of Idaho to rescue her father and his small band.

4   Winnemucca had many names. Her people called her "Mother." Others called her "Princess." Her Paiute name means "shell flower." She herself liked the name "Sarah." But by any name, she was a brave fighter for the rights of her people.

1. Winnemucca was the daughter of
    a. a princess.
    c. a Paiute chief.
    b. a fierce man.
    d. an army scout.

2. The word in the story that means *to save from danger and harm* is

    _____.

3. In paragraph 2, sentence 2, the word *she* means

    _____.

4. The story does not say this, but from what we have read, we can tell that
    a. Winnemucca liked fighting fierce tribes.
    b. Winnemucca was a brave and clever woman.
    c. Winnemucca was afraid of traveling alone.

5. What happened to Winnemucca's father? (Which sentence is exactly like the one in your book?)
    a. Winnemucca's father became a Native American scout.
    b. Winnemucca's father traveled with his band.
    c. Winnemucca's father was taken prisoner.

6. The main idea of the whole story is that
    a. the Paiutes lived in the state of Idaho.
    b. Winnemucca was a leader of her people.
    c. Winnemucca's father lived in a large tribe.

7. The word in paragraph 2, sentence 3, that is the opposite of *few* is

    _____.

8. Which of the following does the story lead you to believe?
    a. People who travel alone like to rescue others.
    b. People can do brave things when they have to.
    c. Living on an army post makes you brave.

Bricks of Sod

1   Pioneers did not begin settling the Great Plains until the late 1800s. Earlier settlers chose not to stay in this region because it was so unfriendly. Since few trees grew there, it seemed impossible to build houses. Because the land was flat and open, there was no protection from the harsh weather. Winters were cold, and heavy snowfall— even blizzards—was common. When the warm weather came, floods and grass fires often followed.

2   Then the cross-country railroads were built. The trains brought farmers to the Great Plains. Since wood was scarce, these settlers couldn't build log cabins to live in. Instead they made houses out of sod. They cut squares of sod, smoothed the edges, and stacked them like bricks. They smoothed the walls and plastered them with clay.

3   The sod houses were very warm. Their thick walls kept out the wind. And the sod was fireproof. The settlers had found the perfect material for their houses!

1. The land on the Great Plains was covered with
   a. sod.   c. trees.
   b. grass.   d. settlers.

2. The word in the story that means *rare* is _____.

3. The word *they* in paragraph 2 means _____.

4. The story does not say this, but from what we have read, we can tell that
   a. the settlers liked sod houses better than brick houses.
   b. winters in the Great Plains are cold but without much snow.
   c. the Great Plains probably didn't have many large rocks.

5. How did settlers get to the Great Plains? (Which sentence is exactly like the one in your book?)
   a. The trains brought farmers to the Great Plains.
   b. The settlers traveled west in wagon trains.
   c. The cross-country railroads led settlers to the Great Plains.

6. The main idea of the whole story is that
   a. when you don't have logs, you can build with sod.
   b. the settlers made good use of the resources at hand.
   c. sod houses are warmer and drier than log cabins.

7. The word in paragraph 3, sentence 2, that is the opposite of *thin* is
   _____.

8. Which of the following does the story lead you to believe?
   a. People in the Great Plains today still live in sod houses.
   b. Early farmers in the Great Plains had a hard life.
   c. When settlers needed supplies, they took the train to town.

The City That Grew in a Lake

1   The center of a lake is a strange place to build a city. Yet this is what the Aztec Indians of Mexico did more than 600 years ago. One of their legends said the people would see an eagle holding a snake in its mouth. When they did, they were to build a city on that spot. They did this, even though the spot was a swampy island in the middle of a lake.

2   The Aztecs had to work hard to build their island city. Much of the water had to be drained. Then canals had to be built. The Aztecs used wooden boards as bridges across the canals.

3   Later, the Aztecs built big, wide roads raised above the water. They also built tall towers of stone. The towers rose high above the canals.

4   In 1519, the island city was the Aztec capital. It has changed very much over the years. But the ancient Aztec city is still a capital. We know it as Mexico City, the great capital of Mexico.

1. The Aztec Indians built a city in the middle of a
   a. mountain. c. desert.
   b. lake. d. river.

2. The word in the story that means *old stories or beliefs passed on down the years* is _____.

3. The word *they* in paragraph 3 means the _____.

4. The story does not say this, but from what we have read, we can tell that
   a. a city made of towers will not last.
   b. cities do not change much over the years.
   c. people can build a city almost anywhere.

5. What is the name of the Aztec city now? (Which sentence is exactly like the one in your book?)
   a. We know it as Mexico City, the great capital of Mexico.
   b. We know it as New York City, the great capital of New York.
   c. We know it as Island City, the great capital of Mexico.

6. The main idea of the whole story is that
   a. everyone should always listen to eagles in Mexico.
   b. the Aztecs built a city in the middle of a lake.
   c. snakes could talk to the Aztec Indians of Mexico.

7. The word in paragraph 4, sentence 1, that is the opposite of *country* is _____.

8. Which of the following does this story lead you to believe?
   a. The Aztecs were very fine builders.
   b. The Aztecs could not do anything well.
   c. The Aztecs used canals instead of roads.

The King Would Not Listen

1   Pierre was very poor, but he had to pay many taxes. He paid taxes to the king and to the church. He paid taxes on his land and the crops he grew. He even paid a tax for being born.

2   Pierre was a peasant in France in the 1780s. Life for all peasants was very hard. The king and the nobles hunted where they pleased. Often the peasants' crops were destroyed under the feet of the nobles' racing horses.

3   Life had always been this way under the rulers and nobles of France. Then those with new ideas began to speak out. They said the people should be free. They said a free people should rule themselves.

4   The king and the nobles would not listen to these new ideas. But Pierre and the other peasants listened. They liked what they heard. Soon they were ready to fight for these new ideas. In 1789 they began the French Revolution.

5   The new ideas changed France. They helped change other countries, too.

1. Pierre lived in
   - a. England.
   - b. America.
   - c. Germany.
   - d. France.

2. The word in the story that means *money paid by people to their government* is _____ .

3. The story says: "Pierre was very poor, but *he* had to pay many taxes." The word *he* means _____ .

4. The story does not say this, but from what we have read, we can tell that
   - a. Pierre did not like to go out and hunt.
   - b. the king did not care how the people lived.
   - c. the peasants thought the nobles should rule.

5. What did Pierre and the other peasants like? (Which sentence is exactly like the one in your book?)
   - a. They liked what they heard.
   - b. They liked the king's horses.
   - c. They liked to fight new ideas.

6. The main idea of the whole story is that
   - a. French kings and nobles liked to destroy crops.
   - b. the peasants of France had to fight to be free.
   - c. poor people like to pay taxes on their land.

7. The word in paragraph 3, sentence 1, that is the opposite of *death* is _____ .

8. Which of the following does this story lead you to believe?
   - a. People will fight for what they believe.
   - b. No one ever has a new idea that works.
   - c. Taxes were paid for the racing horses.

The Salt March

1   In India, in 1930, a small gentle man led thousands of people on a "salt" march. The man was Gandhi (gän′dē). His followers called him *Mahatma* (mə hät′mə). Mahatma means "Great Soul." The Mahatma led his followers 200 miles to the sea. There they made salt by boiling water from the ocean.

2   There had been a salt tax in India for hundreds of years. It was not a fair tax, for the tax was the same for rich and poor. It was one of the most hated taxes in India.

3   India had been ruled by many different people. In 1930, India was still owned and ruled by England. Gandhi wanted his country to be free. But he did not believe in using force. He wanted a peaceful change. His salt march told England and the world that Indians wanted to rule their land themselves.

4   Mahatma Gandhi worked in many ways to free India. In 1947, after almost a hundred years of English rule, India did become a new and free nation.

1. Mahatma Gandhi led his followers to the
   a. pond.   c. lake.
   b. river.   d. sea.

2. The word in the story that means *people who believe in and follow the ideas of a man* is _____ .

3. The word *it* in paragraph 2 means the _____ _____ .

4. The story does not say this, but from what we have read, we can tell that
   a. many people of India loved Gandhi.
   b. Indian people did not like salt.
   c. the salt tax was a very good tax.

5. What did Gandhi want for his country? (Which sentence is exactly like the one in your book?)
   a. Gandhi wanted more salt for his country.
   b. Gandhi wanted his country to be free.
   c. Gandhi wanted only a peaceful march.

6. The main idea of the whole story is that
   a. the hated salt tax was only for the poor people.
   b. Gandhi helped India to get change without force.
   c. all the people wanted to swim in the saltwater.

7. The word in paragraph 1, sentence 1, that is the opposite of *rough* is _____ .

8. Which of the following does this story lead you to believe?
   a. Gandhi's salt march made the people thirsty.
   b. Force is not the only way to get freedom.
   c. The Indians liked to drink ocean water.

The Day King John Could Not Forget

1   It was June 15 in the year 1215. It was a day King John of England was never to forget. On this day, King John signed a paper. The paper was the Magna Carta. It brought about many changes in England.

2   Before this day, King John had always done as he pleased. Both rich and poor suffered under this cruel and greedy king. At last, the nobles and leaders of the church rebelled against the king. They got together and forced King John to sign the Magna Carta. It was the first time the rights of any of the people were put down on paper.

3   The Magna Carta took away some of the king's power. It also said that people were to be judged by others like themselves, and not by the king.

4   The nobles and the others were thinking of themselves. But later, the Magna Carta became part of English law. The law was not only for the rich, but for all the people of England.

1. The day King John could not forget was in
   a. 1512.
   c. 1492.
   b. 1215.
   d. 1968.

2. The word in paragraph 4, sentence 3, that means *a rule made by the government* is _____ .

3. The story says: "Before this day, King John had always done as *he* pleased." The word *he* takes us back to _____ .

4. The story does not say this, but from what we have read, we can tell that
   a. King John was a good king for all the people.
   b. it is bad for one person to have too much power.
   c. all the people in England were rich and happy.

5. What did the Magna Carta do? (Which sentence is exactly like the one in your book?)
   a. It brought about many changes in England.
   b. It brought many people to stay in England.
   c. It was the first paper King John signed.

6. The main idea of the whole story is that
   a. the Magna Carta did not change anything at all.
   b. the Magna Carta gave the English important rights.
   c. the Magna Carta gave the rulers more power than before.

7. The word in paragraph 2, sentence 2, that is the opposite of *kind* is _____ .

8. Which of the following does this story lead you to believe?
   a. Laws should be the same for all people.
   b. All English rulers are cruel and greedy.
   c. The nobles never thought of themselves.

Spin-offs All Around You

1   A spin-off isn't a game. It's not a dance step either. A *spin-off* is something extra that grows from a new idea or a new science. Many things that make our lives better are spin-offs from space science.

2   In order to send humans and rockets into space, we had to find special ways to do things. We needed materials that would not burn or become soft when very hot. We also needed ways to keep astronauts healthy.

3   A blast-off causes a gust of 5,000-degree heat. A coating made to protect launch pads from heat is now painted on our bridges. It is also found in cars, trucks, and heating pipes. Another coating made to protect rocket parts is used on eyeglasses. It keeps the glasses from getting scratched.

4   NASA has developed tools to check astronauts' hearts while in space. These tools now help doctors make sure our own hearts are healthy.

5   Space science does more than teach us about distant planets. It helps make life on Earth better for everybody.

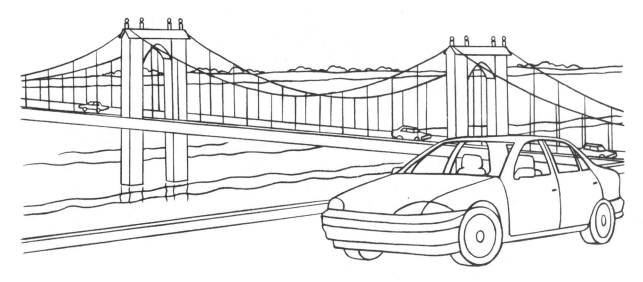

1. Many things first made for use in space are now used by
    a. space scientists.   c. painters.
    b. astronauts.   d. people on Earth.

2. The word in the story that means *to keep safe* is _____.

3. The word *it* in paragraph 5 means _____.

4. The story does not say this, but from what we have read, we can tell that
    a. people who develop spin-offs need to know a lot about science.
    b. astronauts need to wear glasses when they are in space.
    c. doctors go along on space missions to keep astronauts healthy.

5. How hot does it get when a rocket is launched? (Which sentence is exactly like the one in your book?)
    a. The launch pad heats up to over 5,000 degrees.
    b. A blast-off causes a gust of 5,000-degree heat.
    c. A blast-off causes the launch pad to burn.

6. The main idea of the story is that
    a. there are no new ways to do things now.
    b. space science can add to everyday lives.
    c. it is easy for the human body to adapt to life in space.

7. The word in paragraph 4, sentence 2, that is the opposite of *sick* is _____.

8. Which of the following does the story lead you to believe?
    a. Space science has not taught us very much about distant planets.
    b. We have gotten only a few new products through spin-offs.
    c. There are possibilities of spin-offs from sciences other than space science.

The Engine for Space

1   The automobile engine runs very well on the ground. Inside the engine, fuel is mixed with air and burned. The oxygen in the air helps the fuel burn. The air is drawn in from outside.

2   Many airplanes have jet engines. The jet engine also draws in air from the outside. The jet fuel is mixed with the air and burned. Again, the oxygen in the air helps the fuel burn. The burning gases race out the back of the engine. The jet airplane moves ahead.

3   An automobile engine could not take you on a ride through space. A jet engine would not work, either. Both engines need the oxygen that is in air. But there is no air in space. Rocket engines are the only engines that can be used in space.

4   Rocket engines carry their own oxygen. The oxygen and rocket fuel are mixed together inside the rocket. The burning gases race out the back. The rocket shoots ahead.

5   When people travel into space, they must use a rocket engine.

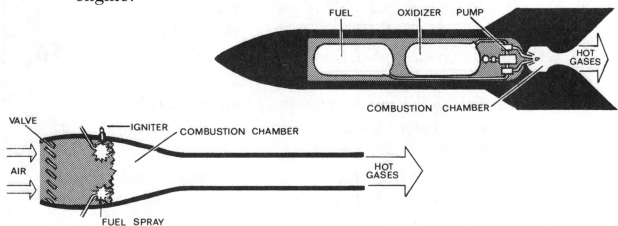

58

1. Oxygen in the air helps fuel
   a. burn.   b. cool.   c. glow.   d. move.

2. The word in the story that means *material burned in an engine* is

   _____ .

3. The story says: "When people travel into space, *they* must use a

   rocket engine." The word *they* means _____ .

4. The story does not say this, but from what we have read, we can
   tell that
   a. someday automobiles will fly to other planets.
   b. jet airplanes can fly backward or forward.
   c. oxygen is needed for many different kinds of engines.

5. Where is there no air? (Which sentence is exactly like the one in
   your book?)
   a. But there is no air in the engine.
   b. But there is no air in space.
   c. But there is no air in a rocket.

6. The main idea of the whole story is that
   a. oxygen and rocket fuel do not mix.
   b. rocket engines are not like car engines.
   c. rocket engines could be used on bicycles.

7. The word in paragraph 2, sentence 6, that is the opposite of

   behind is _____ .

8. Which of the following does the story lead you to believe?
   a. The rocket is the last design possible in engines.
   b. Someday we may have an engine newer than the rocket
      engine.
   c. An automobile engine could fly if it could carry its own
      gasoline.

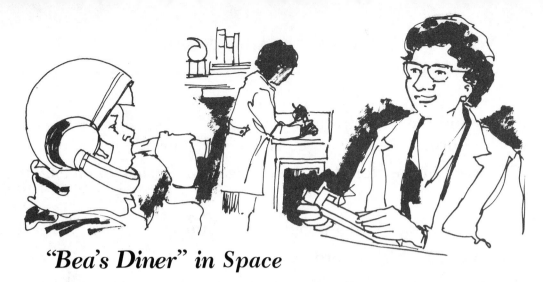

"Bea's Diner" in Space

1   There are special problems in eating in space. Long before John Glenn's first flight, doctors began to plan for space feeding. They called on Beatrice Finkelstein to design food tests. She spent long hours of research on the problems of eating in space.

2   Bea thought if the astronauts got bored, they might make mistakes in flight. She believed that if the astronauts ate delicious food, they would not get as bored. In 1962, John Glenn was placed in orbit. High over Nigeria, he ate Bea's special dinner. On later flights, Bea gave all the Mercury astronauts fancy meals in toothpaste tubes.

3   The astronauts' food is cooked and frozen before they get it. All the water is removed. In the space capsule, the astronauts put the water back into the food.

4   Astronauts cannot drink water from open cups. The water would float in drops in the air. The water is put into a special gun. The astronauts "shoot" the water into their mouths.

5   Eating in space is not easy. Astronauts must learn to eat this way.

1. The astronauts drink water from
   a. lunch boxes.   c. special guns.
   b. closed bags.   d. cups.

2. The word in the story that means *a man or a woman who flies in space* is _____ .

3. The story says: "She thought if the astronauts got bored, *they* might make mistakes in flight." The word *they* means

   _____ .

4. The story does not say this, but from what we have read, we can tell that
   a. you get much hungrier in space than you do on earth.
   b. you cannot have water to drink in a space capsule.
   c. astronauts must learn many new and different things.

5. Why can't astronauts drink water from cups? (Which sentence is exactly like the one in your book?)
   a. The water would float in drops in the air.
   b. The water would spill all over their food.
   c. The water is frozen in the cups.

6. The main idea of the whole story is that
   a. there is more food and water in space than on earth.
   b. eating and drinking in space is a special problem.
   c. astronauts can never eat or drink in a spaceship.

7. The word in paragraph 4, sentence 2, that is the opposite of

   sink is _____ .

8. Which of the following does the story lead you to believe?
   a. Food for astronauts must be made a special way.
   b. Astronauts will only drink water in cups.
   c. All meat on earth comes frozen.

The Man Who Saved the Moon

The old man put on his nightshirt and his nightcap. He was ready to go to bed, but first he wanted a drink of water.

"How thirsty I am! I must have some water," the old man said. He picked up the pitcher from the table near his bed. But it did him no good, for there was no water in the pitcher.

"Wife! Wife!" the old man shouted. "Fetch me some water from the well." But his wife did not hear him, for she was already asleep. "I guess I will just have to get water from the well myself," the old man said. He put his slippers on, went out of the house and walked through the grass to the well. The yellow moon was so bright in the sky, the old man did not need to light his way.

There was a low stone wall around the well. Over the well a bucket hung from an iron hook. A long rope was tied to the hook. The bucket could be put down the well and raised when the rope was pulled.

"I am so thirsty," the old man said, "I wish I could just lean over and drink from the well." The old man leaned over and looked at the water. At once he forgot how thirsty he was for something terrible had happened! The moon was at the bottom of the well!

"Heaven help us!" the old man shouted. "The moon has fallen into the well! Wife! Wife! Come and help me." But his wife did not answer, for she was still sleeping. "I will just have to get the moon out by myself," the old man said. "What would the world be like without a moon?"

The old man took the bucket off the hook and dropped the hook down into the well. He began to pull on the rope, but the hook caught against one of the stones that lined the well and would not come up.

"What a heavy moon!" the old man thought as he pulled. His nightcap slid down over one eye. "Moon," he called out, "you push and I will pull very hard at the same time." The old man pulled and pulled. Suddenly the hook flew out of the well. It hit the old man and knocked him down. He lay flat on the ground with his nightcap over his eyes. Little stars seemed to fly around his head. At last, he took the nightcap off his head, and looked at the sky. Then he began to shout, "I've done it! I've done it!" For up above, the yellow moon was shining brightly in the sky.

"What a wonderful thing I have done," the old man laughed. "I gave the moon such a pull that it flew all the way back into the sky. Without my quick thinking, the world would never have seen the moon again."

The old man got up and started to walk back to the house. He was so excited, he forgot how thirsty he was. "I must wake up my wife and tell her how I've saved the moon! And tomorrow I shall tell everybody about the moon in the well. Tomorrow the whole world will know about the man who saved the moon."

580 words

II

Environment Affects All Living Things

In this section, you will read about how environment effects people, plants, and animals. You will read about these things in the areas of anthropology, biology, Earth science, ecology, economics, geography, history, and space.

Keep these questions in mind when you are reading.

1. What things in nature make up our environment?

2. How does the world around you affect you?

3. Can you control your environment?

4. If you cannot control the environment around you, what can you do about it?

5. Can an environment be changed? How?

Look on pages 8-10 for help with words in this section you don't understand.

A Virus Among Us

1   Chicken pox is no joke. Every year, from 1 1/2 to 2 million people in the United States come down with the disease. Most of the people who get it are children.

2   Chicken pox is caused by a virus. A virus is a tiny form of living matter that can be seen only with a microscope. Viruses can grow only in the living tissue of plants, animals, or people. The virus that causes chicken pox lives in saliva and mucus. When people get the virus they cough and sneeze. This is how the virus is spread to other people.

3   People with chicken pox get an itchy rash. It takes from one to three weeks before the rash appears. During this time, they can spread the disease to other people without knowing it.

4   Until recently, it was very hard to avoid getting chicken pox. Finally, in 1995, the U.S. government approved a chicken pox vaccine. If all young children get the vaccine, a time will come when most people will be safe from chicken pox.

FIND THE ANSWERS

1. People with chicken pox get a
   - a. vaccine.
   - c. rash.
   - b. tissue.
   - d. microscope.
2. The word in the story that means *sickness* is _____.
3. The word *they* in paragraph 3 means _____.
4. The story does not say this, but from what we have read, we can tell that
   - a. adults don't get chicken pox.
   - b. people with chicken pox don't feel well.
   - c. the chicken pox virus can grow in dirt.
5. How long does it take for the chicken pox rash to appear? (Which sentence is exactly like the one in your book?)
   - a. It takes about a week before the rash appears.
   - b. It takes about a month for the rash to appear.
   - c. It takes from one to three weeks before the rash appears.
6. The main idea of the whole story is that
   - a. if you eat the right things, you won't get chicken pox.
   - b. there's not much people can do to avoid catching chicken pox.
   - c. chicken pox is very common, but thanks to a new vaccine, it will probably disappear.
7. The word in paragraph 2, sentence 2, that is the opposite of *huge* is

   _____.
8. Which of the following does the story lead you to believe?
   - a. If one child in the class gets chicken pox, many other children are likely to get it.
   - b. People who go out in the rain without raincoats are likely to get chicken pox.
   - c. Most children get chicken pox by the time they are seven.

A Refrigerator in the Ground

1   It can be difficult to build on the frozen land of the Arctic. The heat from a building will melt the frozen soil and turn it into mud. When a building is constructed on ground that is not firm, the building will begin to sink.

2   The frozen soil of the Arctic is called permafrost. When engineers plan to build on it, they look for a spot with rock under the ground. They remove the permafrost above the rock. Rock has no water in it, so it cannot freeze. If it cannot freeze, it cannot melt.

3   A building was constructed in this way in Greenland. However, after a while, people noticed that one side of the building was getting lower. Engineers found that what had looked like rock was really permafrost. The permafrost was melting, and that corner of the building was sinking. The engineers decided to put refrigerator coils into the ground. The coils would keep the soil frozen all the time. So you might say, the inside of a refrigerator is holding up a building!

1. The heat from a building can make frozen soil
    a. grow.   c. colder.
    b. melt.   d. rocky.

2. The word in the story that means *frozen soil* is
    _____.

3. The word *they* in paragraph 2 means _____.

4. The story does not say this, but from what we have read, we can tell that
    a. engineers often need to find new ways of doing things.
    b. engineers do not need to know much about permafrost.
    c. the engineers in Greenland are nice people.

5. Why doesn't rock freeze? (Which sentence is exactly like the one in your book?)
    a. Rock is too large to freeze.
    b. Rock has no water in it, so it cannot freeze.
    c. Rock cannot get cold enough to freeze.

6. The main idea of the whole story is that
    a. people cannot build in Greenland.
    b. most buildings need refrigerator coils.
    c. it is not easy to build in the Arctic.

7. The word in paragraph 1, sentence 1, that is the opposite of *easy* is
    _____.

8. Which is the following does the story lead you to believe?
    a. Large building often sink.
    b. Engineers can solve construction problems.
    c. If a building is sinking, it must be torn down.

The Strangers

1   More than a thousand years ago, some people known as Maoris (mä′ō rēz) lived in Polynesia (pol′ə nē′zhə). Polynesia is a group of many small islands in the Pacific Ocean. These islands are warm and pleasant.

2   Why would people leave islands like these and sail off for another land, where everything would be strange and new? No one knows, but this is what the Maoris did. They left their islands and sailed across the Pacific in canoes. They landed in New Zealand, more than a thousand miles away.

3   Life in New Zealand was very different. The Maoris had to learn to hunt new animals for food. They had to learn to weave flax into cloth. They had to learn many new things to stay alive in the new land.

4   Maoris still live in New Zealand. But they have not forgotten they came as strangers. One of their dances tells how the Maoris sailed the ocean to find their new home. Maoris today still remember that they came from another land long ago.

FIND THE ANSWERS

1. The islands of Polynesia are in the
    - a. Indian Ocean.
    - b. Atlantic Ocean.
    - c. Pacific Ocean.
    - d. Arctic Ocean.

2. The word in the story that means *a plant that people use to weave linen cloth* is _____.

3. The story says: "Maoris still live in New Zealand. But *they* have not forgotten they came as strangers." The word *they* means

    _____.

4. The story does not say this, but from what we have read, we can tell that
    - a. people dance all the time in New Zealand.
    - b. people should never leave their own country.
    - c. people can make a new life in a strange land.

5. Where did the Maoris go? (Which sentence is exactly like the one in your book?)
    - a. They landed in New Zealand, more than a thousand miles away.
    - b. They landed in New Zealand far across the Pacific.
    - c. They landed in New Zealand in canoes only one mile away.

6. The main idea of the whole story is that
    - a. New Zealand was a cold and unpleasant country.
    - b. the Maoris came from Polynesia to New Zealand.
    - c. the Maoris found New Zealand was like Polynesia.

7. The word in paragraph 4, sentence 2, that is the opposite of *remembered* is _____.

8. Which of the following does this story lead you to believe?
    - a. The old Maoris were good sailors.
    - b. From Polynesia you can see New Zealand.
    - c. The Maoris have forgotten their history.

Not Made for Swimming

1   The flamingo is a beautiful water bird with bright pink or red feathers. Over many thousands of years, the flamingo has adapted to the place where it lives. Its legs changed. Its neck and bill changed, too.

2   The flamingo gets all its food from the water. Its neck is long and thin, which helps the bird reach the water more easily. Its bill is long and bent. Around the edge of the bill is a small fringe. This fringe lets in all the small plants and animals that the flamingo eats. But it keeps mud and water out of the bird's mouth.

3   Many water birds are fine swimmers. But the legs of the flamingo are not made for swimming. They are long and thin and look like stilts. The flamingo does not swim out into deep water. It wades close to the shore. Flamingo legs are fine for wading!

4   The flamingo may seem strange to us. But if it had not adapted to the place where it lives, it would have died out.

72

1. The flamingo is
   a. a fish.   c. a duck.
   b. a plant.   d. a bird.

2. The word in the story that means *a bird's mouth* is

   _____ .

3. The story says: "Over many thousands of years, the flamingo has adapted to the place where *it* lives." The word *it* means

   _____ .

4. The story does not say this, but from what we have read, we can tell that
   a. the flamingo can fly better than most birds.
   b. the flamingo could not live away from water.
   c. all birds like to wade in the water today.

5. What shape is the flamingo's bill? (Which sentence is exactly like the one in your book?)
   a. Its bill is short and straight.
   b. Its bill is long and bent.
   c. Its bill is long and curved.

6. The main idea of the whole story is that
   a. the flamingo has adapted to where it lives.
   b. birds with long legs live longer than others.
   c. all wading birds have long, thin bills.

7. The word in paragraph 3, sentence 5, that is the opposite of

   far is _____ .

8. Which of the following does the story lead you to believe?
   a. Most birds have long legs.
   b. Birds adapt very quickly.
   c. Not all waterbirds swim well.

The Animal That Keeps to Itself

1   Someday, if you are lucky, you may see a bongo. But the only way most people will see it is in a zoo. Bongos belong to the antelope family. They are found in Africa, where they live deep in forests. Even in Africa, very few people ever get to see a bongo. The bongo does not come out of the forests very often. It is an animal that keeps to itself.

2   The bongo has beautiful coloring. Its hair is a bright brown mixed with orange and red. Down its back and across its sides the bongo has yellow-white stripes.

3   Animals that hunt at night usually have big eyes. This helps them see better at night. The forests in which the bongos live are very dark. The eyes of the bongos are very big. The bongo has adapted its way of living to the darkness.

4   Bongos in zoos do not like to go outside on bright days. They only go outside on those days when it is dark or very cloudy.

1. Bongos live in
   a. Africa.   c. Alaska.
   b. Algeria.   d. Argentina.

2. The word in the story that means *a group of related animals* is

   _____ .

3. The story says: "The bongo does not come out of the forests very often. *It* is an animal that keeps to itself." The word *it* means

   _____ .

4. The story does not say this, but from what we have read, we can tell that
   a. bongos would have trouble on the open plains.
   b. bongos hunt in the daytime with other animals.
   c. bongos eat only plants that grow in jungles.

5. To what family do the bongos belong? (Which sentence is exactly like the one in your book?)
   a. Bongos belong to the small deer family.
   b. Bongos belong to the zebra family.
   c. Bongos belong to the antelope family.

6. The main idea of the whole story is that
   a. most bongos want to live in the zoo.
   b. bongos are lucky to have such big brown eyes.
   c. the bongo is a strange forest animal of Africa.

7. The word in paragraph 4, sentence 2, that is the opposite of

   sunny is _____ .

8. Which of the following does the story lead you to believe?
   a. Most people never get to Africa.
   b. No bongos have ever been captured.
   c. Sunny days are best for visiting bongos in zoos.

Traveler's Friend

1   Most plants would die under the hot desert sun. They could not live without water. But the cactus is not like other plants. It lives very well in the desert.

2   The roots of the cactus spread out near the top of the ground. Sometimes rain falls in the desert. Then the roots of the cactus take the water in quickly. The water goes into the thick, cactus stem. The water stays in the stem for a long time. The stem is like a storage tank. Even if it does not rain for months, the cactus does not die. It gets the water it needs from its own storage tank!

3   There are different kinds of cactus plants. They may be small, or tall as trees. The giant saguaro (sə gwär′ō) often grows as high as 50 feet. The barrel cactus sometimes grows six feet high. This cactus can store water in its stem for years. It has been called the "traveler's friend," since people traveling in the desert can get water from it.

FIND THE ANSWERS

1. The "traveler's friend" is the
   - a. saguaro cactus.
   - b. barrel cactus.
   - c. pincushion cactus.
   - d. strawberry cactus.

2. The word in the story that means *very large* or *huge* is

   _____ .

3. The story says: "But the cactus is not like other plants. *It* lives

   very well in the desert." The word *it* means _____ .

4. The story does not say this, but from what we have read, we can
   tell that
   - a. cactus plants never grow tall.
   - b. all travelers like to rest under cactus plants.
   - c. the barrel cactus is taller than most plants.

5. Where is water stored in the cactus plant? (Which sentence is
   exactly like the one in your book?)
   - a. The water goes into the thick, cactus stem.
   - b. The water goes into the thick, cactus leaves.
   - c. The water is stored in the large flowers.

6. The main idea of the whole story is that
   - a. most plants can live long under the hot desert sun.
   - b. the cactus can live in the desert by storing water.
   - c. some plants do not need water to grow in the desert.

7. The word in paragraph 2, sentence 8, that is the opposite of

   gives is _____ .

8. Which of the following does the story lead you to believe?
   - a. Water can only be stored for a few days.
   - b. Even cactus plants need some rain.
   - c. The giant saguaro is never taller than six feet.

Digging to Learn

1   Women and men who learn all about the earth and its rocks are called geologists. Some geologists study the earth's history to learn how the earth got to be as it is. Others want to know how the earth can be used. They find ways to save our soil and our water. They help to plan cities, roads, and bridges.

2   Geologists have a motto that says, "With mind and hammer." Geologists often carry small hammers. When they are in the field, they break off pieces of rock. They take the rocks home and study them. By learning about the kinds of rocks in a place, geologists can put together the history of an area. They can tell whether an ocean covered the land. They can tell if the weather was hot or cold, wet or dry.

3   Through the work of geologists, we have maps that show us how the land and water look today. Other maps show us how the world was long ago. Geologists are the people who tell us about our earth.

FIND THE ANSWERS

1. Some geologists help to plan
   - a. schools.
   - c. roads.
   - b. houses.
   - d. stores.

2. The word in the story that means *the ground* or *dirt* is

   _____ .

3. The word *it* in sentence 2 means the _____ .

4. The story does not say this, but from what we have read, we can tell that
   - a. geologists cannot break any rocks.
   - b. rocks can tell the story of earth.
   - c. all rocks are exactly the same.

5. What do geologists do? (Which sentence is exactly like the one in your book?)
   - a. They find ways to save our soil and our water.
   - b. They break bridges with their small hammers.
   - c. They use new ways to destroy our soil and water.

6. The main idea of the whole story is that
   - a. geologists study the earth and its history.
   - b. geologists use their hammers to make our roads.
   - c. the ocean once covered the land.

7. The word in paragraph 2, sentence 1, that is the opposite of

   without is _____ .

8. Which of the following does this story lead you to believe?
   - a. All geologists study the same thing.
   - b. Rocks are not important to geologists.
   - c. The work geologists do is important.

Life from the Past

1   Long ago, Alice Wilson was known in her Canadian home as the "rock doctor." The lowlands near her home were rich in rocks and fossils. Alice became an expert on the fossils buried in the limestone there.

2   Mary Ann Anning was a young woman who lived in England nearly 200 years ago. She loved to go out after storms had torn at the cliffs near her home. There she would find rocks that had been washed down in the rain. She always found some fossil treasures on these hunts.

3   When she was twelve years old, Mary found some strange bones. They formed a skeleton that was almost perfect. The people of the town thought they had belonged to a great dragon. But scientists learned that the skeleton was a kind of giant dinosaur that lived on the earth millions of years ago.

4   Today scientists are still studying Mary's "fish-lizard." They call it *Ichthyosaurus*. That was the first dinosaur fossil Mary found. But it wasn't her last. She found many more unknown things. Mary was famous in her own time. Early geologists like Mary Ann Anning and Alice Wilson gave us clues about life in the past.

FIND THE ANSWERS

1. Fossils are found in
    - a. dragons.
    - b. rocks.
    - c. treasures.
    - d. giants.

2. The word in the story that means *the bones or imprint of something that lived long ago* is _____.

3. The story says, "That was the first dinosaur fossil Mary found. But *it* wasn't her last." The word *it* takes us back to the word

    _____.

4. The story does not say this, but from what we have read, we can tell that
    - a. all skeletons are found on cliffs.
    - b. geologists never study skeletons.
    - c. skeletons can last for a long time.

5. How well known was Mary? (Which sentence is exactly like the one in your book?)
    - a. Mary was famous in her own time.
    - b. No one knew what Mary was doing.
    - c. Mary is very famous today.

6. The main idea of the whole story is that
    - a. We can study past ages through fossils.
    - b. Hunting fossils is a good way to make money.
    - c. Geologists like to hunt in the rain.

7. The word in paragraph 4, sentence 5, that is the opposite of *lost* is _____.

8. Which of the following does this story lead you to believe?
    - a. Fossils can become dragons.
    - b. All women should be geologists.
    - c. People can learn a lot about things close to home.

Call a Geologist

1   A tunnel is being built through a mountain. If it is dug through weak, soft rock, the tunnel may fall in. If the diggers strike water, the tunnel will be flooded. If the rock is too hard, workers will not be able to dig through it. Before a tunnel can be built, people must know what they will find. They call in a geologist. She or he helps plan a tunnel so it can go through rock that is dry and hard, but not too hard.

2   A steel and concrete skyscraper is going up. A skyscraper cannot be built over sand or mud. Sand and mud cannot hold up a building. Before a skyscraper can be built, people must know what lies under the surface of the earth. They call in geologists.

3   Geologists find the best places to build dams and bridges. They look for the best places to dig wells for water. Geologists help us make wise use of the land.

1. Geologists find the best places to build
   a. weak, soft rock.   c. sand and mud.
   b. land.   d. dams and bridges.

2. The word in the story that means *a hard building material* or *cement* is _____.

3. The story says: "If the rock is too hard, workers will not be able to dig through *it*." The word *it* means _____.

4. The story does not say this, but from what we have read, we can tell that
   a. tunnels should not go through mountains.
   b. people can only guess where to build dams and bridges.
   c. planning is needed before a tunnel is built.

5. Where can a skyscraper not be built? (Which sentence is exactly like the one in your book?)
   a. A skyscraper cannot be built over solid ground.
   b. A skyscraper cannot be built over very hard rock.
   c. A skyscraper cannot be built over sand or mud.

6. The main idea of the whole story is that
   a. tunnels can be built through any kind of soil.
   b. geologists help us make wise use of the land.
   c. a skyscraper is built on very hard rock.

7. The word in paragraph 3, sentence 3, that is the opposite of *foolish* is _____.

8. Which of the following does the story lead you to believe?
   a. Geologists are not important for dam building.
   b. Skyscrapers are one-story buildings.
   c. Digging a tunnel can be very dangerous.

Feet Like Snowshoes

1   The tundra is a frozen land near the Arctic Ocean. Most of the year it is covered with ice and snow. For six months the tundra is dark. The sun seems to be hiding.

2   One of the few animals that can live in this cold dark land is the caribou. The caribou's thick fur keeps it warm. Indians and other hunters in the tundra often used caribou hides as sleeping bags. The caribou's feet move across the deep snow like snowshoes. Always on the move, caribou travel in long lines looking for food.

3   From May to July, the tundra springs to life. The sun shines. Snow and ice melt. The top of the ground becomes soft and wet. Small plants make the land bright with color. Birds come, and insects fill the air with busy sounds. Small arctic animals look for food.

4   By August the tundra begins to grow cold. In September snow covers the ground once more. Soon the tundra again becomes a white world under a dark sky.

FIND THE ANSWERS

1. The tundra is land near
   - a. the mountains.
   - b. the equator.
   - c. the Indian Ocean.
   - d. the Arctic Ocean.

2. The word in sentence 5 that means *a kind of deer* is

   _____ .

3. The word *it* in paragraph 2 means the _____ .

4. The story does not say this, but from what we have read, we can tell that
   - a. trees do not grow on the tundra.
   - b. many people live on the tundra.
   - c. the tundra is warm most of the year.

5. How does the caribou get through deep snow? (Which sentence is exactly like the one in your book?)
   - a. The caribou's feet sink into the deep snow of the tundra.
   - b. The caribou travels a long way to find birds and insects.
   - c. The caribou's feet move across the deep snow like snow-shoes.

6. The main idea of the whole story is that
   - a. many kinds of animals can live on the tundra.
   - b. the tundra is a land with a long, dark winter.
   - c. many people visit the tundra in the winter.

7. The word in paragraph 2, sentence 3, that is the opposite of

   waking is _____ .

8. Which of the following does this story lead you to believe?
   - a. Animals have had to adapt to living on the tundra.
   - b. It is easy for the caribou to find food in winter.
   - c. August is the warmest month on the tundra.

The Land of Dripping Water

1   High overhead, monkeys swing by their tails and parrots call out. Nearer the ground, birds fly through the air. Climbing cats and other animals hunt for food. Snakes slide along the ground. A thousand insects go about their work. Trees seem to reach up to the sky. Their big green leaves are 200 feet above the ground. This is a rain forest.

2   The rain forest is hot and wet. About 90 inches of rain fall each year. Even in the "dry season" three or four inches of rain fall each month. The large leaves of the trees catch the rain as it falls. The water drips slowly to the ground. It keeps on dripping long after the rain has stopped. But wind and sun never reach the forest floor.

3   The big trees protect the life living under them. Their flowers are food for insects. Birds and small animals stay under the leaves where they are safe from high-flying eagles. The monkeys live on nuts and fruit from the trees.

1. In the dry season of a rain forest the monthly rainfall may be
   a. over 90 inches.   c. three or four inches.
   b. 200 feet.   d. less than an inch.

2. The word in the story that means *a special time of the year, like summer or winter,* is _____ .

3. The story says: "The water drips slowly to the ground. *It* keeps on dripping." The word *it* means the _____ .

4. The story does not say this, but from what we have read, we can tell that
   a. there are no flowers in a rain forest.
   b. the rain falls to the ground fast.
   c. there is little light in a rain forest.

5. What catches the rain as it falls? (Which sentence is exactly like the one in your book?)
   a. The big trees catch the rain as it falls.
   b. The large leaves of the trees catch the rain as it falls.
   c. The water is caught in ponds on the floor of the forest.

6. The main idea of the whole story is that
   a. many things live and grow in a rain forest.
   b. too many birds live near the ground.
   c. there are many insects living in a rain forest.

7. The word in paragraph 1, sentence 1, that is the opposite of *underneath* is _____ .

8. Which of the following does this story lead you to believe?
   a. An eagle can't live near a rain forest.
   b. A rain forest would be beautiful to see.
   c. A rain forest would be completely quiet.

Everglades or <u>Neverglades</u>!

1   On January 10, 1997, the restoration of the Everglades began with a celebration. An important group of children joined in.

2   The Everglades is one of the biggest swamps in the world. It covers more than one million acres in Florida. Many of the plants and animals there are not found anyplace else.

3   In 1906, Florida began to drain the Everglades to make farmland. Forty years later people finally realized the importance of the Everglades, and in 1947 part of it was made into a National Park. But this did not stop the damage. As more and more people moved into the area, water was drained off the swamp for household use. Farmers used chemicals on their crops that poisoned the water in the swamp. Wild animals began to die.

4   Many people became worried and joined together to try and restore water to the Everglades. One group that helped was the Young Friends of the Everglades. Its members wrote letters, put on programs, and helped plant sea oats, which help to stop erosion. That is why these children were at the celebration. They carried a banner saying, "Everglades or <u>Neverglades</u>."

FIND THE ANSWERS

1. The Everglades is in
   a. Florence.   b. Europe.   c. Africa.   d. Florida.
2. The word in the story that means *soft, wet land* is _____.
3. The word *their* in paragraph 3, sentence 5, means _____.
4. The story does not say this, but from what we have read, we can tell that
   a. Florida farmers have learned how to grow crops in swamps.
   b. children are more concerned about the environment than adults are.
   c. the Everglades National Park is an interesting place to visit.
5. When and why did the damage to the Everglades begin? (Which sentence is exactly like the one in your book?)
   a. In 1906, Florida began to drain the Everglades to make farmland.
   b. The Everglades has been in trouble since 1947, when farmers moved there.
   c. The damage to the Everglades began about 40 years ago because of the rare animals.
6. The main idea of the whole story is that
   a. once a place changes nothing can be done about it.
   b. many kinds of plants and animals live in the Everglades.
   c. people working together can make a difference.
7. The word in paragraph 2, sentence 3, that is the opposite of *lost* is

   _____.

8. Which of the following does this story lead you to believe?
   a. Alligators used to live in the Everglades, but they don't live there anymore.
   b. The Everglades would be a good place to study animals.
   c. Crocodiles can live only in fresh water.

The Machine That Hatches Eggs

1   Peck, peck, peck! An egg is about to hatch. A baby chick will soon break through its shell. This baby chick will never see the mother hen. It is hatching inside an incubator with hundreds of other eggs. An incubator is an egg-hatching machine.

2   The air inside the incubator is kept at about 100 degrees day and night. Every four to six hours, the machine turns the eggs over. In twenty-one days, nine out of ten eggs will hatch. The people who raise these chicks take orders from farmers ahead of time. They can be sure the chicks will be ready.

3   Eggs left in a hen's nest do not hatch so well. Sometimes the hen leaves the nest. The eggs grow cold. Sometimes the eggs are broken or taken by another animal.

4   Incubators are not a new idea. Even in early Egypt, eggs were taken from the mother hen. They were kept warm until they hatched. Today, electric heat is used. Millions of eggs are hatched in incubators each year.

FIND THE ANSWERS

1. The air inside the incubator is kept at about
   a. 50 degrees all night.
   b. 20 degrees all day.
   c. 1000 degrees during the day.
   d. 100 degrees day and night.

2. The word that means *to break out of an egg* is _____ .

3. The story says: "This baby chick will never see the mother hen. *It* is hatching inside an incubator with hundreds of other eggs."

   The word *it* means _____ .

4. The story does not say this, but from what we have read, we can tell that
   a. hens lay eggs in their hatches in their cold nests.
   b. incubators hatch eggs better than hens do.
   c. incubator chicks live with the mother hen.

5. What kind of heat is used in incubators today? (Which sentence is exactly like the one in your book?)
   a. Today, the heat of the sun is used.
   b. Today, electric heat is used.
   c. Today, heat from fire is used.

6. The main idea of the whole story is that
   a. incubators are used to hatch eggs.
   b. baby chicks do not have a mother.
   c. incubators are a very new idea.

7. The word in paragraph 2, sentence 3, that is the opposite of

   won't is _____ .

8. Which of the following does this story lead you to believe?
   a. The incubator helps the farmer's business.
   b. A good hen can hatch twice as many eggs as an incubator.
   c. An incubator can only hold two dozen eggs.

When the Rains Didn't Come

1   People think of the climate of an area as unchanging. They expect the weather to be about the same year after year. But a climate can change and when that happens, life changes for the people. For example, if the climate becomes bad for farming, farmers must find other work or move on.

2   In the 1930s, there was a terrible change in the climate in the American Southwest. Long periods went by without any rain. These droughts were followed by powerful winds that blew dried-out soil into the air. People had to wear masks on their faces to protect themselves from the flying dust. The area became known as the Dust Bowl.

3   It became impossible to farm the land. Jobs were scarce, so farmers could not find other work. People had to leave their homes. In Arkansas and Oklahoma, over 350,000 people moved away. They piled their belongings into old cars and trucks, then they went west in search of jobs. They could not live on land that had changed so greatly.

1. In the American Southwest, there were long periods without
   a. wind.　　b. sun.　　c. clouds.　　d. rain.

2. The word in the story that means *the kind of weather in an area* is

   _____.

3. The word *their* in paragraph 3 means _____.

4. The story does not say this, but from what we have read, we can
   tell that
   a. people were sad to leave their homes.
   b. people in Arkansas and Oklahoma never liked to farm.
   c. the people who left their homes had plenty of money.

5. Why did farmers have to leave the Dust Bowl? (Which sentence is
   exactly like the one in your book?)
   a. It became impossible to buy food.
   b. It became impossible to farm the land.
   c. It became impossible to wear masks on their faces.

6. The main idea of the whole story is that
   a. the American Southwest was called the Dust Bowl.
   b. environment affects the way people make a living.
   c. people had to wear masks because of the dust in the air.

7. The word in paragraph 1, sentence 2, that is the opposite of
   different is _____.

8. Which of the following does this story lead you to believe?
   a. The weather is very important to a farmer's life.
   b. Farmers can control the weather.
   c. Nobody can earn a living when there is not enough rain.

A Day in May

1   It is a hot day. You go to an air-conditioned building. You feel better. The air conditioning makes the July day seem like a day in May.

2   People have been trying to keep cool in hot weather for thousands of years. In ancient Egypt, people put wet mats over their doors. When the wind blew through the mats, it cooled the air inside the houses.

3   In the 1500s, the first fans were used. They were better than wet mats. But they did not cool the air very much. Today, with air conditioning, we can control the temperature inside.

4   Air conditioning helps us in many ways. In hospitals, anesthetics used in the operating rooms sometimes exploded because of the humidity in the air. Air conditioning controls humidity. It also keeps the air in the operating rooms clean. In some deep mines, the temperature is very high. It is too hot to work. Air conditioning brings the heat to a safe working temperature.

FIND THE ANSWERS

1. In ancient Egypt, over their doors people put
   - a. wet mats.
   - b. fans.
   - c. ice.
   - d. cold water.

2. The word in the story that means *the measure of how hot or cold something is* is _____ .

3. The word *they* in paragraph 3 means the first _____ .

4. The story does not say this, but from what we have read, we can tell that
   - a. few people are comfortable in hot weather.
   - b. wet mats make the best air conditioners.
   - c. even today fans are better than air conditioning.

5. Does air conditioning help us? (Which sentence is exactly like the one in your book?)
   - a. Air conditioning helps us in many ways.
   - b. Air conditioning cannot help us at all.
   - c. Air conditioning only helps us in winter.

6. The main idea of the whole story is that
   - a. the best way to keep cool is with a fan.
   - b. air conditioning keeps us from working in summer.
   - c. air conditioning helps us control temperatures.

7. The word in paragraph 4, sentence 7, that is the opposite of *dangerous* is _____ .

8. Which of the following does this story lead you to believe?
   - a. Today, we are able to control temperatures outside.
   - b. In the 1500s, people had air conditioning.
   - c. People cannot do their best work on a very hot day.

Halfway Country

1   If there were more rain on the prairie, trees would grow. If there were less rain, the land would be a dry desert. As it is, grass grows there very well. The weather is neither too hot nor too dry. We might call the prairie "halfway country."

2   The first settlers pushing west found this halfway land covered with grass. They saw that grass grew well, so they planted wheat, which belongs to the grass family.

3   In 1861, Kansas became one of the states of the prairie. In Kansas, winter wheat grows well. The seed is planted in the fall. Cattle can feed on the young plants in the winter. In the spring, they are moved. The wheat grows tall for harvesting in summer. A field of winter wheat gives a larger crop than spring wheat. Spring wheat is planted in spring. It is harvested the same summer. Farmers in Kansas plant only winter wheat.

4   Kansas grows more wheat than any other state. This state is sometimes called the "Breadbasket of America."

FIND THE ANSWERS

1. According to the story, wheat is a kind of
   - a. season.
   - b. seed.
   - c. grass.
   - d. tree.

2. The word in the story that means *a flat land with few trees where grass grows well* is _____ .

3. The story says: "Spring wheat is planted in spring. *It* is harvested the same summer." The word *it* means _____ .

4. The story does not say this, but from what we have read, we can tell that
   - a. no grass grows in the prairies.
   - b. wheat is used in making bread.
   - c. the prairie is hot and dry.

5. What kind of wheat gives a larger crop? (Which sentence is exactly like the one in your book?)
   - a. A field of spring wheat gives a larger crop in the dry desert.
   - b. A field of winter wheat gives a larger crop than spring wheat.
   - c. Spring wheat and winter wheat will give the same size crops.

6. The main idea of the whole story is that
   - a. wheat grows well in the prairie state of Kansas.
   - b. a lot of bread is made in the Kansas breadbasket.
   - c. there are a lot of trees in the state of Kansas.

7. The word in paragraph 2, sentence 1, that is the opposite of *pulling* is _____ .

8. Which of the following does this story lead you to believe?
   - a. Wheat makes good baskets.
   - b. We have only one prairie state.
   - c. Many wheat farmers also raise cattle.

Have an Apple!

1   The United States is one of the great fruit-growing countries in the world. Fine red apples come from orchards in Washington and New York. Golden oranges come from Southern California and Florida. Fruit grows in all parts of America. The kind of fruit that is grown depends on the weather in each place.

2   Orange trees cannot be grown where temperatures drop below freezing. Southern California and Florida are far apart, but their weather is much the same. They do not often have freezing temperatures.

3   In Washington, apple trees were planted near the Pacific Ocean. In New York, they grow near the Great Lakes. Apple trees are often planted near water. Water temperature changes more slowly than land temperature. Near water, the temperature does not drop as fast. There is less chance of frost in late spring or early fall. Frost can kill apples.

4   Our country has many kinds of weather. It has many kinds of soil. Because of this, we raise and eat more fruit than any other country in the world.

FIND THE ANSWERS

1. Near water, the temperature changes
   a. faster.   c. not at all.
   b. slower.   d. the same as elsewhere.

2. The word in the story that means *places where fruit trees grow*
   is _____.

3. The story says: "Our country has many kinds of weather. *It* has
   many kinds of soil." The word *it* means our _____.

4. The story does not say this, but from what we have read, we can
   tell that
   a. most fruits grow anywhere in the United States.
   b. freezing temperatures are good for fruit.
   c. the same fruit can grow in different places.

5. How fast does water temperature change? (Which sentence is
   exactly like the one in your book?)
   a. Water and land temperature change at exactly the same
      rate.
   b. Water temperature changes more slowly than land
      temperature.
   c. Water temperature changes faster than land temperature.

6. The main idea of the whole story is that
   a. orange trees usually grow where it is cold.
   b. different fruits grow in different weather.
   c. the cold cannot kill oranges and apples.

7. The word in paragraph 2, sentence 1, that is the opposite of
   boiling is _____.

8. Which of the following does this story lead you to believe?
   a. The fruit we buy comes from many places.
   b. Orange trees are often planted near water.
   c. The soil is about the same in all the states.

More than a Million Cows

1   Once there were no cows in America. Cows were brought here in the 1600s by English settlers.

2   A good cow gives about a thousand gallons of milk a year. She seems to be eating all the time. In the summer, she eats the grass from two acres of ground. In a year's time, she eats about 11 tons of feed. She drinks about 3,000 gallons of water each year. It is easy to see why cows must be raised where there is plenty of grass and water.

3   In the Great Lakes Plains in southern Wisconsin, the land is rich. The season for good crops lasts a long time. There is plenty of water. It is a good place to raise cattle. Its grasslands and cattle have made Wisconsin the leading dairy state in the United States.

4   There are more milk cows in Wisconsin than in any other state. Wisconsin has almost 1 1/2 million dairy cows!

FIND THE ANSWERS

1. Once there were no cows in
   a. Australia. c. Amsterdam.
   b. America. d. Africa.

2. The word in the story that means *people who came from other countries to live in America* is _____.

3. The story says: "A good cow gives about a thousand gallons of milk a year. *She* seems to be eating all the time." The word *she* means

   _____.

4. The story does not say this, but from what we have read, we can tell that
   a. in America, cows are found only in Wisconsin.
   b. cows don't eat grass in southern Wisconsin.
   c. cows cannot be raised on all types of land.

5. How much milk does a good cow give a year? (Which sentence is exactly like the one in your book?)
   a. A good cow gives about a thousand gallons of milk a year.
   b. A good cow gives about a hundred gallons of milk a month.
   c. A good cow gives about two gallons of milk a week.

6. The main idea of the whole story is that
   a. cows need plenty of grass and water.
   b. there are more cows than people in America.
   c. cows do not belong in America anymore.

7. The word in paragraph 3, sentence 1, that is the opposite of *northern* is _____.

8. Which of the following does the story lead you to believe?
   a. Native Americans kept cows before the settlers came.
   b. Wisconsin is a desert state.
   c. Americans drink a lot of milk.

A Way to Remember

1   From earliest times, people have had a need to keep some kind of record. In a record, you put down something you want to remember. People want those who come after them to remember the old customs. A way of doing things by most people in the same tribe or country is called a custom.

2   Native Americans who were experts at tanning hides were very proud. They kept records of their good work. An expert tanner would place a dot on the handle of her scraping tool for every robe she tanned. When she had 100 dots, she made a raised circle at the end of the tool.

3   In one part of the country, it became a custom to draw pictures on tepees. Some drawings were about the families in each tepee. Other drawings told about battles. In another part of the country, Native Americans used wampum on deerskin belts. Wampum are shell beads. Stories were told with designs of different colored beads. Tribes using wampum this way could read these stories.

1. In a record, you put down something you want to
   - a. forget.
   - b. sing.
   - c. remember.
   - d. draw.

2. The word in the story that means *a kind of tent in which Indians lived* is _____ .

3. The word *she* in paragraph 2 means the expert

   _____ .

4. The story does not say this, but from what we have read, we can tell that
   - a. a custom is something made out of animal skin.
   - b. people have worked out many ways to keep records.
   - c. no one wants to remember the old customs.

5. How did Native Americans show their pride in their tanning work? (Which sentence is exactly like the one in your book?)
   - a. They made bead designs as copies.
   - b. They kept records of their good work.
   - c. They paid for it in wampum.

6. The main idea of the whole story is that
   - a. the Native Americans kept records.
   - b. Indians told a lot of stories.
   - c. People do not like to keep records.

7. The word in paragraph 1, sentence 1, that is the opposite of *latest* is _____ .

8. Which of the following does this story lead you to believe?
   - a. Only people who can write can keep records.
   - b. Native Americans invented records.
   - c. Different people have different customs.

History on Strings

1   Ancient people had different ways of keeping records. In South America, it was the custom for the Inca Indians to use *quipus* (kē'püz). The quipus were made up of many strings hanging from one long rope or crossbar.

2   Knots of different sizes and shapes were tied in the strings. The size and shapes meant different things. The color of each string was important. So was its place on the crossbar.

3   With quipus, records were kept of the number of people, of the hours they worked, and of the food they grew. Messages, laws, even stories and poems, were "written" on quipus. Great happenings in the history of their people were also written on the quipus.

4   Not everyone knew what the quipus said. Children had to have special training. They had to learn how to make the knots. They had to learn what the different knots and strings said. It often took as long as four years for them to learn all these things.

FIND THE ANSWERS

1. The Inca Indians lived in
   a. South America.   c. the United States.
   b. Canada.   d. Europe.

2. The word in the story that means *a record of what has happened in the past* is _____.

3. The story says: "Children had to have special training. *They* had to learn how to make the knots." The word *they* means

   _____.

4. The story does not say this, but from what we have read, we can tell that
   a. everyone could read the records on the quipus.
   b. quipus were toys made by the Inca.
   c. without records legends might be lost.

5. What were tied in the strings? (Which sentence is exactly like the one in your book?)
   a. Crossbars were tied in the strings by the Inca Indians.
   b. Colored beads of different sizes were tied in the strings.
   c. Knots of different sizes and shapes were tied in the strings.

6. The main idea of the whole story is that
   a. all Inca children learned to write on quipus.
   b. the Inca kept records on quipus.
   c. the Inca grew food called quipus.

7. The word in paragraph 1, sentence 1, that is the opposite of *losing* is _____.

8. Which of the following does the story lead you to believe?
   a. All quipus looked exactly the same.
   b. It was hard to learn to read quipus.
   c. Most children learned all about quipus in a year.

The Writing on Leaves

1   What country do you live in? In what century do you live there? Both of these things make a difference in how you live! Suppose you had been born in ancient Mexico. You would be an Aztec Indian. You would know nothing about printing machines. You could not sit down and read a book. You would not even have an alphabet.

2   We know much about the Aztec Indians from stories they wrote. How could they write the history of their people? They used pictures and designs to tell of the things that happened to them. Sometimes they drew their pictures and designs in books made of deerskin. Other times, a special kind of paper was used. This paper was made from leaves of the agave (ə gā′vē) plant.

3   The Aztec books would not look like books to you. Their books were either rolled or folded. We call these rolled books scrolls. A few of these Aztec scrolls can be found in some of our museums.

1. The Aztec Indians lived in
   a. Argentina.   c. California.
   b. Mexico.   d. Peru.

2. The word in the story that means *rolls of paper with writing on them* is _____ .

3. The story says: "We know much about the Aztec Indians from stories *they* wrote." The word *they* means _____ .

4. The story does not say this, but from what we have read, we can tell that
   a. it is not easy to read stories told in designs.
   b. the agave plant had paper leaves that were rolled.
   c. the deerskin books did not last a very long time.

5. What special kind of paper did the Aztec Indians use? (Which sentence is exactly like the one in your book?)
   a. This paper was made from leaves of the agave plant.
   b. This paper was made from leaves of the pepper plant.
   c. This paper was made from deerskin in ancient Mexico.

6. The main idea of the whole story is that
   a. the Aztec Indians left no books or records.
   b. people long ago didn't need history.
   c. Aztec Indians left a record of their history.

7. The word in paragraph 1, sentence 2, that is the opposite of *here* is _____ .

8. Which of the following does this story lead you to believe?
   a. A scroll is a kind of printing machine.
   b. Many different peoples have felt the need to keep records.
   c. Many Aztec scrolls remain for us today.

Only 26 Million Miles Away

1   Venus is our nearest neighbor in space. At times, it is only 26 million miles away. We know that in some ways Venus is like Earth. Like our own planet, Venus goes around the sun. It is almost the same size as Earth, too.

2   In other ways, the two planets are very different. Venus lies under thick clouds of dust. The clouds hold the sun's heat under them. In some places, the temperature goes up to 536 degrees. Rain never falls on Venus the way it does on Earth and there are no oceans there.

3   Venus has been visited by more spacecraft than any other planet. Each voyage teaches us new facts about Venus. The *Magellan* spacecraft began mapping Venus in 1990. It has mapped almost all of the surface. The maps show that Venus is covered with mountains and volcanic rock.

FIND THE ANSWERS

1. In some places on Venus the temperature goes up to
   a. 500 degrees.
   b. 563 degrees.
   c. 536 degrees.
   d. 635 degrees.

2. The word in the story that means *a heavenly body that goes around the sun* is _____.

3. The word *it* in paragraph 1 means _____.

4. The story does not say this, but from what we have read, we can tell that
   a. most planets are more than 26 million miles away from Earth.
   b. Venus is a cool planet with a great deal of water.
   c. the planet Venus goes around Earth twice each year.

5. Where does Venus lie? (Which sentence is exactly like the one in your book?)
   a. Venus lies in the sun's heat and dust.
   b. Venus lies under thick clouds of dust.
   c. Venus lies under thick white rain clouds.

6. The main idea of the whole story is that
   a. Venus is very different from Earth.
   b. it is interesting to explore the planets.
   c. there is too much water on Venus today.

7. The word in paragraph 3, sentence 3, that is the opposite of *ended* is _____.

8. Which of the following does the story lead you to believe?
   a. Venus is much smaller than Earth.
   b. The air on Venus must be much like that on Earth.
   c. People from Earth could not live on Venus.

The Mysteries of Mars

1   Is there life on Mars? We still do not know. Since the Viking probes, we are sure that earthlike people do not live on Mars. Earth people need oxygen to breathe. There is almost no oxygen on Mars.

2   Living on Mars would be like living on a very high mountain. There would be little air. It might be 50 degrees above zero at noon and 100 degrees below zero at night.

3   Many people used to think there could be plants on Mars. We now know that Mars has very little carbon. Carbon is a kind of material found in all plants and animals on earth. Through a telescope, Mars looks red. In some places, it seems gray. At times, the gray color turns gray-green, then brown, then gray again. People once thought this suggested that plant life changed color with the seasons.

4   Today we know that the red color comes from a fine dust of iron on the planet. Scientists are still working to explain some of the changing colors. Mars has many mysteries left.

1. To breathe, earth people need
   a. water.
   b. shelter.
   c. oxygen.
   d. masks.

2. The word in paragraph 4, sentence 3, that means *things which are unexplained* is _____ .

3. The story says: "Through a telescope, Mars looks red. In some places, *it* seems gray." The word *it* means _____ .

4. The story does not say this, but from what we have read, we can tell that
   a. someday we may know why the colors change on Mars.
   b. plants grow very easily on Mars.
   c. we know that people on Mars wear red clothing.

5. What does Mars look like through a telescope? (Which sentence is exactly like the one in your book?)
   a. Mars looks red at times through a telescope.
   b. Through a telescope, Mars looks red.
   c. Mars looks gray, then brown through a telescope.

6. The main idea of the whole story is that
   a. there is much to learn about Mars.
   b. earth people could live on Mars.
   c. Mars turns different colors.

7. The word in paragraph 3, sentence 1, that is the opposite of *few* is _____ .

8. Which of the following does this story lead you to believe?
   a. Some earth people have already visited Mars.
   b. There is a lot of oxygen on Mars.
   c. There may be strange discoveries on Mars.

Work Clothes for Space

1   When NASA found a problem with the Hubble space telescope, astronauts went into space to repair it. Before they went to work, they put on their work clothes. The space suits they wore made it possible for them to stay alive.

2   There is no air in outer space, so the astronauts wore backpacks to give them oxygen. There is no air pressure either, so the oxygen in the backpack was also used to pressurize the suit.

3   The temperature in outer space can go from over 200 degrees below zero to almost 250 degrees above zero. When the temperature dropped, the pressurized suits kept the astronauts warm. When the temperature went up, they were glad to be wearing special long underwear. The underwear kept them cool because it had tubes with cool water running through them.

4   The space suits were like one-person spacecraft. Wearing them, the astronauts were inside an environment much like the one they knew on Earth.

FIND THE ANSWERS

1. The temperature in space can get as low as 200 degrees
    - a. above zero.
    - c. below freezing.
    - b. below zero.
    - d. above freezing.
2. The word in the story that means *a gas we breathe* is _____.
3. The word *them* in paragraph 3 means _____.
4. The story does not say this, but from what we have read we can tell that
    - a. astronauts cannot move around in space suits.
    - b. astronauts in space suits cannot pick up small things.
    - c. space suits are quite comfortable.
5. Why was the astronauts' underwear important? (Which sentence is exactly like the one in your book?)
    - a. The underwear kept them cool because it had tubes with cool water running through them.
    - b. The underwear made it possible to breathe because of the oxygen in the tubes.
    - c. The underwear warmed them up when the temperature went down below 250 degrees.
6. The main idea of the whole story is that
    - a. space suits make it possible for humans to stay alive in outer space.
    - b. space suits are the latest fashion on Earth.
    - c. it can be dangerous working in a space suit.
7. The word in paragraph 1, sentence 2, that is the opposite of *play* is _____.
8. Which of the following does the story lead you to believe?
    - a. Repairing the Hubble space telescope was fairly easy.
    - b. The astronauts did not need to wear helmets while they made the repairs.
    - c. Astronauts need to keep their space suits on when they are inside a spacecraft.

The Wise Father

Once there was a mouse who searched everywhere to find a husband good enough for his only daughter. His daughter was a very beautiful mouse. Her fur was silvery-gray and very silky. Her eyes were large and bright and her tail was very slender and graceful.

"Who is good enough to marry our beautiful daughter?" the mouse asked his wife.

"She should marry the sun," said the wife.

"True!" said the father mouse. "The sun is the most powerful thing in the world. Only the sun is good enough for our daughter."

The mouse climbed up in the sky to talk to the sun.

"Oh, Great Sun," he said, "you may marry my daughter, since you are the most powerful thing in the world."

"Thank you for the honor," said the sun, "but see

how the clouds can hide my face. I cannot shine through a cloud, so a cloud must be more powerful than I am."

The mouse thought about this and decided it must be true. So he went to a very large cloud that was passing across the sky.

"Oh, Great Cloud," he said, "you may marry my daughter, since you are so very powerful."

"Something else is more powerful than I am," said the cloud. "Feel the wind. The wind pushes me all about the sky. I cannot go where I want to. I have to go where the wind pushes me."

The mouse thought about this for a little while. He decided that the wind must be greater than the cloud so he ran very fast across the sky until he caught up with the wind.

"Oh, Great Wind," said the mouse, "you may marry my daughter, since you are so powerful. Nothing can stop you. You must be the greatest thing in the world."

"Not I," said the wind. "See that wall? That wall stops me. I blow and blow and blow, but I cannot push the wall out of my way. I cannot break through it."

The mouse thought for a little while and decided this was true. So he dropped down out of the sky and went to the wall.

"Oh, Great Wall," said the mouse, "you may marry my daughter, since you are so strong. You can stop the wind, even when it blows very hard."

"That is true enough," said the wall, "and yet I cannot stop a mouse. A mouse can nibble and gnaw at me till he makes a hole. Then he passes through. A mouse must be more powerful than I am. Perhaps your daughter should marry a mouse."

"What a splendid idea!" said the mouse. "I never thought of that!" So he went back home again where he found a handsome young gentleman mouse with long whiskers for his daughter to marry. This made the daughter very happy.

"You have found the perfect husband for me," she said. "What a wise father you are!"

500 words

116

III

People Use the Resources at Hand

In this section you will read about the use of things that we have available to us. You will read about these things in the areas of biology, Earth science, ecology, economics, geography, history, mathematics, political science, and space science.

Keep these questions in mind when you are reading.

1. What are five things that are useful to me?

2. From where did they come?

3. How would my life be without them?

4. Is there danger of losing or running out of these things?

5. What can I do to keep from losing those things that are useful to me?

Look at pages 10-12 for help with words in this section you don't understand.

Prizes for Maria

1   Maria Martinez of San Ildefonso liked to make pottery. In 1908, some people came to New Mexico to study the Native Americans living there. They saw the pottery that Maria had made. They thought it was very beautiful. They asked her to copy pottery made by her ancestors.

2   Many potters use a wheel. They put the clay on a circle that spins around. As the clay turns, they push it into the shape they want. American Indians like Maria do not use a wheel. They roll their clay into long ropes like a snake. They wind the ropes to build sides. While the clay is wet, they press the ropes together. They paint the pottery in colors made from ground-up rocks. They bake the pottery over beds of hot coals.

3   Maria found a way to make black pottery. It was different from pottery found anywhere else in the world. Maria made pottery for more than fifty years. She used only material found near her home. Her pottery became famous. She won prizes from the United States and other countries.

FIND THE ANSWERS

1. Maria Martinez lived in
   - a. California.
   - b. New Mexico.
   - c. Utah.
   - d. Arizona.

2. The word in the story that means *bowls or pots made of clay* is

   _____.

3. The story says: "Maria made pottery for more than fifty years. *She* only used material found near her home." The word *she* means

   _____.

4. The story does not say this, but from what we have read, we can tell that
   - a. the early people could not make pottery well.
   - b. some American Indians still make pottery the old way.
   - c. anyone can win a prize for old pottery.

5. How do the American Indians color their pottery? (Which sentence is exactly like the one in your book?)
   - a. They paint the pottery in colors made from ground-up rocks.
   - b. They paint the pottery in colors made from coal.
   - c. They paint the pottery in colors made from chalk.

6. The main idea of the whole story is that
   - a. Maria used a wheel to make pottery.
   - b. the American Indians made clay snakes.
   - c. a native girl made very fine pottery.

7. The word in paragraph 2, sentence 5, that is the opposite of *unroll*
   is _____.

8. Which of the following does the story lead you to believe?
   - a. Most Americans do not like pottery.
   - b. It is easy to make black pottery.
   - c. Fine American Indian pottery is admired throughout the world.

The Holy Grounds

1   The year was 1836. A white man had entered the land of the Sioux in Minnesota. He was an artist who was a good friend to the Native Americans. But the Sioux almost killed him, for he had entered their "holy grounds." These holy grounds were quarries. A quarry is a place from which stone is dug or cut. The red stone in these quarries had been used by the Sioux for more than 300 years. The Sioux were famous for the pipes they carved from this stone.

2   Pipes played a big part in the lives of Native Americans. Pipes were smoked after special ceremonies, and they were passed around when tribes made peace with each other. Pipes made from the "holy ground" were very important. The Native Americans thought the smooth red stone came from the bodies of their ancestors.

3   Today, the quarries are the Pipestone National Monument. Only the Sioux may use stone from these quarries. They still make and carve pipes from their "holy grounds."

FIND THE ANSWERS

1. The "holy grounds" of the Sioux were
   - a. mountains.
   - b. churches.
   - c. quarries.
   - d. parks.

2. The word in sentence 8 that means *shaped by cutting out* is

   _____.

3. The word *he* in sentence 3 means the same as _____.

4. The story does not say this, but from what we have read, we can tell that
   - a. all quarries of red stone are holy to Native American tribes.
   - b. quarries are made out of pipes found on monuments.
   - c. the white man did not know the quarries were holy.

5. What is a quarry? (Which sentence is exactly like the one in your book?)
   - a. A quarry is a place from which stone is dug or cut.
   - b. A quarry is a place from which stones are carved.
   - c. A quarry is a place where American Indians look for red bones.

6. The main idea of the whole story is that
   - a. the pipestone quarries were holy to the Sioux.
   - b. the Sioux buried their ancestors in quarries.
   - c. the Sioux smoked their pipes in the quarries.

7. The word in paragraph 1, sentence 3, that is the opposite of *enemy* is _____.

8. Which of the following does the story lead you to believe?
   - a. What is holy to some may not be holy to others.
   - b. The Sioux played their pipes in the holy grounds.
   - c. Pipes were not important to Native American tribes.

From the Head of a Whale

1   How do Native Americans make baskets?

2   The Inuit north of the Arctic Circle are whale hunters. They make baskets from baleen. Baleen, which is almost like bone, comes from the head of a whale. The Inuit cut the baleen into long, thin pieces. The baskets have tops made of ivory. The ivory comes from the tusks of walruses.

3   In California, the Washoe Indians make baskets out of bird feathers. The Washoe made feather baskets long before the new settlers came. The Hoopa Indians make baskets of many colors from white grass, fern roots, and fine branches. In Mississippi, the Choctaw Indians make baskets of sugar cane.

4   In New Mexico, the Hopi Indians make baskets from desert plants. They use grass and long, thin yucca leaves. Other Hopi use wild bushes and weeds. Some baskets are so well made that they will hold water.

5   The Native Americans use the best material they can find near their homes. Each kind of basket tells us something about the place where the particular tribe lives.

122

1. Hopi Indians live in
   a. California.   c. Florida.
   b. Mississippi.   d. New Mexico.

2. The word in paragraph 5 that means *something from which other things are made* is _____.

3. The story says: "Some baskets are so well made that *they* will hold water." The word *they* takes us back to the word _____.

4. The story does not say this, but from what we have read, we can tell that
   a. baskets are useful and needed by many people.
   b. the Native Americans like to build houses of baleen.
   c. people always made their baskets of feathers.

5. Where does the ivory come from? (Which sentence is exactly like the one in your book?)
   a. The ivory comes from the Choctaw Indians.
   b. The ivory comes from the bones of walruses.
   c. The ivory comes from the tusks of walruses.

6. The main idea of the whole story is that
   a. Native Americans are the only people who will weave baskets.
   b. baskets are used only by tribes in Mississippi.
   c. Native Americans make baskets of those materials at hand.

7. The word in paragraph 5, sentence 1, that is the opposite of *worst* is

   _____.

8. Which of the following does the story lead you to believe?
   a. Only Hopi Indians catch whale bones in baskets.
   b. Native American baskets were not very well made.
   c. People today greatly admire the basketmakers.

Food for Tomorrow

1   Algae (al'jē) are plants that have no roots or leaves. They grow in wet places. You may have seen algae on top of the water in a pond or lake. Algae will even grow in fish bowls. Most algae are green or blue-green, but some are red, brown, or black.

2   Often, you buy algae at the drugstore, but you do not know it. Some kinds of algae are used in making ice cream, toothpaste, skin creams, and medicine.

3   Algae do not look or taste good, but they are high in food value. They can be made into flour. Women and men are working to make algae taste better. Then they can be used for food.

4   Tomorrow, more people will live in the world. They will need more food to eat. Algae are easy to grow. They may become an important food.

5   Algae can grow on spaceships. The people who go out into space may have their own algae gardens. Then they will not run out of food.

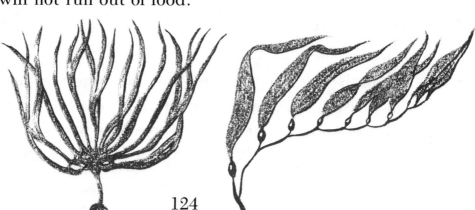

124

FIND THE ANSWERS

1. Algae grow
     a. in drugstores.   c. in dry places.
     b. in wet places.   d. in toothpaste.

2. The word in the story that means *the parts of plants that grow under the ground* is _____ .

3. The story says: "Algae do not look or taste good, but *they* are high in food value." The word *they* takes us back to the word

     _____ .

4. The story does not say this, but from what we have read, we can tell that
     a. algae may help feed the world's people.
     b. algae are good food for fish on spaceships.
     c. algae gardens can only grow in outer space.

5. What are algae? (Which sentence is exactly like the one in your book?)
     a. Algae are vegetables that have tasty roots.
     b. Algae are skin creams grown in the drugstore.
     c. Algae are plants that have no roots or leaves.

6. The main idea of the whole story is that
     a. algae can be dried and spun into thread for clothing.
     b. algae are plants that may become important as food.
     c. people in spaceships today want to start growing gardens.

7. The word in paragraph 3, sentence 3, that is the opposite of *worse*

     is _____ .

8. Which of the following does this story lead you to believe?
     a. Algae are never red.
     b. Algae can grow in small places.
     c. The work on algae has not yet begun.

New Uses for Old Plants

1   Have you ever seen something fuzzy growing on old, damp bread? You may have heard this growth called mold. Mold is a fungus. A fungus is a plant that has no flowers or leaves. Unlike other plants, it cannot make its own food.

2   Molds can be harmful, but people have learned how to use them. One kind of mold is used to help make some cheeses taste good. Another mold is used to change sugar into citric acid. Citric acid has a sour taste. Look for the words "citric acid" on food that you buy. It is used in many foods and drinks.

3   Some molds are used to help fight diseases. Have you ever had a shot of penicillin when you were sick? Penicillin is made from a mold. The Chinese used mold from a vegetable to cure skin diseases more than 3,000 years ago. The ancient peoples of Central America use molds to cure wounds.

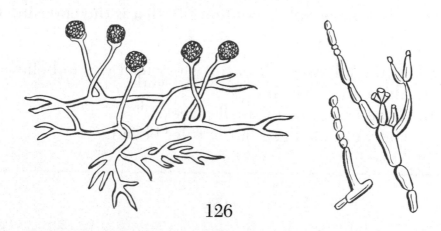

1. Mold is a
    a. flower.   c. fungus.
    b. leaf.   d. root.

2. The word in the story that means *broken or cut places in the body*
    is _____.

3. The story says: "Molds can be harmful, but people have learned
    how to use *them*." The word *them* takes us back to the word
    _____.

4. The story does not say this, but from what we have read, we can
    tell that
    a. some things can be both useful and harmful.
    b. citric acid makes food taste much too sweet.
    c. the Chinese first found penicillin long ago.

5. How is fungus different from most plants? (Which sentence is
    exactly like the one in your book?)
    a. A fungus is a plant that has no roots or petals.
    b. A fungus is a plant that has no flowers or leaves.
    c. A fungus is a plant that has no leaves or branches.

6. The main idea of the whole story is that
    a. only the Chinese use molds.
    b. all molds are harmful plants.
    c. some molds are useful to us.

7. The word in paragraph 1, sentence 5, that is the opposite of *like* is
    _____.

8. Which of the following does the story lead you to believe?
    a. Only in the last few years have molds been put to good use.
    b. There were wise people in ancient China.
    c. Molds are beautiful plants.

Two Plants in One

1   Lichens (lī′kənz) are strange plants. They are the only plants made up of two different kinds of plants. Lichens are made up of algae and fungi. Lichens grow almost anywhere in the world. They can live where other plants die.

2   Most plants will not grow well in sandy soil. Some lichens do very well in this kind of soil. They keep the wind from blowing the soil away. They keep water from washing the soil away.

3   Lichens can help make poor soil rich enough for other plants to grow. Lichens on rocks give off a weak acid. This acid breaks down the minerals in the rocks. After a while, soil forms in the cracks of the rocks. Other plants begin to grow.

4   In Lapland, lichens are used as food for reindeer. In Norway and Sweden, lichens are dried and made into powder. The powder is used in cereals and bread. One lichen that has a sweet smell is used in making perfume. Other lichens are used to color cloth.

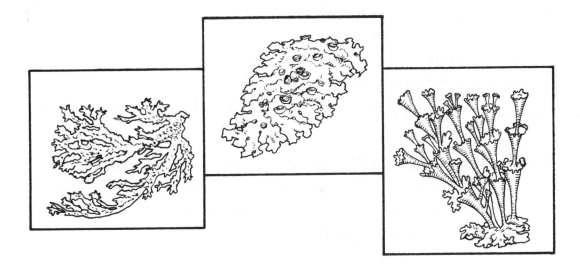

1. In Lapland, lichens are used as food for
    a. reindeer.   c. chickens.
    b. horses.   d. cats.

2. The word in paragraph 3, sentence 3, that means *certain things formed in the earth that are not animal or plant life* is

    _____ .

3. The story says: "Lichens grow almost anywhere in the world. *They* can live where other plants die." The word *they* takes us

back to the word _____ .

4. The story does not say this, but from what we have read, we can tell that
    a. in Lapland, lichens are dried and colored for reindeer.
    b. most lichens make the soil dry so that it blows away.
    c. without help from lichens, some plants could not grow.

5. Where do lichens grow? (Which sentence is exactly like the one in your book?)
    a. Lichens grow only on rocks that have cracks.
    b. Lichens grow almost anywhere in the world.
    c. Lichens grow only where plants are strange.

6. The main idea of the whole story is that
    a. lichens grow in Lapland, Norway, and France.
    b. lichens are important plants in many ways.
    c. lichens are used to color cereals and bread.

7. The word in paragraph 1, sentence 4, that is the opposite of

nowhere is _____ .

8. Which of the following does this story lead you to believe?
    a. Lichens kill other plants.
    b. Lichens are full of minerals.
    c. People make good use of lichens.

What's in a Rock?

1   Look at a rock, and what do you see? Something to build with? Something to eat or wear or keep you warm? Could it once have been an animal or a plant? Does it make you think of treasures hidden under the ground? No? Yet rocks are all these things.

2   The soil in which we grow our food is made up of rock worn down by weather. The salt we put on our food comes from halite. Halite is a natural mineral found as rock.

3   Have you seen walls of limestone in some buildings? Limestone is made up of plants and skeletons of sea creatures that died long ago. The coal that keeps some of us warm in winter comes from plants that lived millions of years ago.

4   Gold and silver and diamonds are called treasures. They are dug from rock. But these are not our only treasures. When you look at a rock, you may see many more of the treasures of our earth.

130

FIND THE ANSWERS

1. Soil is rock worn down by
   - a. minerals.
   - b. salt.
   - c. weather.
   - d. skeletons.

2. The word in sentence 5 that means *not seen* or *kept out of sight* is _____ .

3. The word *it* in sentence 4 takes us back to sentence 1 and the word _____ .

4. The story does not say this, but from what we have read, we can tell that
   - a. coal comes from old limestone.
   - b. all rocks are made of salt.
   - c. there are many kinds of rocks.

5. What are called treasures? (Which sentence is exactly like the one in your book?)
   - a. All the things that we wear are called treasures.
   - b. Gold and silver and diamonds are called treasures.
   - c. Rocks hidden in the ground are called treasures.

6. The main idea of the whole story is that
   - a. people use rocks in many different ways.
   - b. rocks are not very important to us.
   - c. all rocks are hidden under the ground.

7. The word in paragraph 3, sentence 3, that is the opposite of *cool* is _____ .

8. Which of the following does this story lead you to believe?
   - a. Buildings are made of halite and limestone plants.
   - b. People who study rocks can tell much about the earth.
   - c. Gold is made up of the skeletons of sea creatures.

Mirrors from Volcanoes

1   Have you ever seen a hill made of glass? In our country, there is a famous glass hill called Obsidian Cliff. It is in Yellowstone National Park.

2   Hot lava from volcanoes does not look much like glass. But lava that cooled fast and got hard made the natural glass called obsidian.

3   Obsidian is not clear, like window glass. But some fine thin pieces of obsidian seem clear. Most obsidian is black and shiny. Obsidian is also found in other colors.

4   Like glass, obsidian is very easy to break. It breaks into smooth, curved pieces with thin sharp edges. Its sharp edges made it good for knives, arrowheads, and points for spears. The early American Indians used obsidian this way.

5   Early people also used obsidian as a mirror. The Mayan Indians of Mexico had obsidian mirrors. People in other parts of the world had obsidian mirrors, too. Obsidian in colors was sometimes used for ornaments and jewelry as well.

FIND THE ANSWERS

1. Obsidian is natural
   - a. jewelry.
   - b. arrowheads.
   - c. earth.
   - d. glass.

2. The word in the story that means *something in which you can see yourself* is _____.

3. The word *it* in paragraph 4 takes us back to the word
   _____.

4. The story does not say this, but from what we have read, we can tell that
   - a. American Indians never used obsidian.
   - b. lava does not always cool fast.
   - c. obsidian does not have many uses.

5. How did early people use obsidian? (Which sentence is exactly like the one in your book?)
   - a. Early people used obsidian to cool the lava.
   - b. Early people used obsidian only for windows.
   - c. Early people also used obsidian as a mirror.

6. The main idea of the whole story is that
   - a. all obsidian is very black and shiny.
   - b. American Indians used obsidian in different ways.
   - c. obsidian is found only in North America.

7. The word in paragraph 2, sentence 2, that is the opposite of *unnatural* is _____.

8. Which of the following does the story lead you to believe?
   - a. Obsidian must always be used as a mirror.
   - b. Obsidian is just as clear as window glass.
   - c. Obsidian can still be used to make jewelry.

Growing Rocks from Seeds

1   Quartz is one of the most ordinary minerals found on Earth. Some quartz is found in almost every rock, in different shapes and colors.

2   Quartz is used in different ways. Quartz sand is needed to make glass. Because of its many pretty colors, some quartz is made into jewelry.

3   You could not watch your favorite television show or listen to the radio without the help of this mineral. When you turn to a station, you always know where to find it. Quartz keeps each station in its own place on the dial. Today, most watches are made with quartz. The quartz crystals in them keep time by vibrating at a steady rate.

4   Quartz is so useful that people make synthetic quartz crystals. Thin pieces of quartz are used for "seeds." The seeds are put in water in metal cups. The cups are closed for several weeks. They are heated to high temperatures. When the cups are opened, the "seeds" have become perfect crystals. Some crystals grow to weigh almost a pound.

FIND THE ANSWERS

1. Quartz is used to make
     a. ice.   c. rocks.
     b. jewelry.   d. minerals.

2. The word in the story that means *a place that sends out programs on radio or television* is _____.

3. The word *they* in paragraph 4 means _____.

4. The story does not say this, but from what we have read we can tell that
     a. quartz is very hard to find.
     b. quartz is made of ice and sand.
     c. quartz is an important mineral.

5. What happens to the quartz seeds? (Which sentence is exactly like the one in your book?)
     a. The seeds are put in water in metal cups.
     b. The seeds are put in grass in large cups.
     c. The seeds are watered in hot metal cups.

6. The main idea of the whole story is that
     a. quartz has many uses.
     b. quartz is not common.
     c. quartz is pretty.

7. The word in paragraph 2, sentence 3, that is the opposite of *ugly* is
   _____.

8. Which of the following does the story lead you to believe?
     a. Someday, we may run out of natural quartz.
     b. People may find many more uses for quartz someday.
     c. Quartz can only be used to make jewelry.

Fences That Bloom

1   The farmers were planting rosebushes to make a wide fence around their pasture. The rosebushes would keep the cows from getting into the cornfield next door. This fence would also make a home for wildlife.

2   Long ago, forests covered this land. There were many wild animals and birds. Then people came and cleared the land. They cut down the trees and put up wire fences. The animals and birds lost their homes. When the rains came, much of the good soil was washed away. There were no tree roots to hold it back.

3   Today's farmers are trying to put back some of the things that early farmers took away. They are planting fences made of rosebushes. The thick bushes not only keep farm animals in their own pastures. They stop the strong wind from blowing away the soil. Wildlife once again has a place to live. And, of course, fences that bloom in the spring look better than wires across a field!

FIND THE ANSWERS

1. The farmers made a fence of
   a. trees.   c. rosebushes.
   b. flowers.   d. cornstalks.

2. The word in the story that means *something built around or along*

   a field to keep things in or out is _____ .

3. The story says: "When the rains came, much of the good soil was washed away. There were no tree roots to hold *it* back." The word

   it takes us back to the word _____ .

4. The story does not say this, but from what we have read, we can tell that
   a. farm animals only like to eat rosebushes.
   b. farmers now take good care of their soil.
   c. the best place for nests is in wire fences.

5. For whom would this fence also make a home? (Which sentence is exactly like the one in your book?)
   a. This fence would make a home for the farmers.
   b. This fence would make a home for all the cows.
   c. This fence would also make a home for wildlife.

6. The main idea of the whole story is that
   a. some rosebushes make very good fences.
   b. there are too many forests and not enough fences.
   c. strong winds are good for rosebushes.

7. The word in paragraph 2, sentence 1, that is the opposite of

   uncovered is _____ .

8. Which of the following does this story lead you to believe?
   a. People have done much damage to nature.
   b. No one wants to have birds around.
   c. Washed soil is the best kind.

Fish That Climb Ladders

1   Salmon are fish that live along our West Coast. They spend part of their lives in the ocean. Then they swim up the rivers, lay eggs, and die. The eggs hatch, and the young fish make their way back to the ocean. Later, they too go up rivers to make nests and lay eggs.

2   Salmon are strong fish. They are able to swim up very fast rivers. They can jump over small waterfalls. Some salmon jump ten feet into the air.

3   When people built large dams, the fish could not get up the rivers. Again and again, they tried to jump over the dams. Many fish died.

4   Now when high dams are built, fish ladders are built also. The ladders look like big, wide steps beside the dam. There are sometimes as many as eighty steps stretching out over 1,000 feet. Water runs down these ladders. With the help of the ladders, the salmon can jump over the dam one step at a time.

1. Salmon are helped over dams by means of
   a. waterfalls.   c. nests.
   b. feet.   d. steps.

2. The word in the story that means *steps that are used to climb* is

   _____ .

3. The story says: "Salmon are strong fish. *They* are able to swim up very fast rivers." The word *they* means

   _____ .

4. The story does not say this, but from what we have read, we can tell that
   a. salmon would die out if they could not go up rivers.
   b. salmon sometimes build their nests on wide ladders.
   c. salmon can jump much better than they can swim.

5. How high can salmon jump? (Which sentence is exactly like the one in your book?)
   a. Some salmon will only jump a few feet.
   b. Some salmon jump one foot in a river.
   c. Some salmon jump ten feet into the air.

6. The main idea of the whole story is that
   a. fish climb ladders to get food.
   b. people help salmon jump over dams.
   c. salmon never leave the ocean.

7. The word in paragraph 1, sentence 2, that is the opposite of

   whole is _____ .

8. Which of the following does this story lead you to believe?
   a. All dams kill fish.
   b. People want to take care of salmon.
   c. Salmon live only in the ocean.

The Brown Snow

1   The brown snow fell in New England in 1936. The snow had turned brown from the dust in the air. The dust came from the plains states, 1,600 miles away.

2   Wheat and too many cattle had destroyed the land. When the first settlers reached the plains, they had found short, thick grass. They raised cattle. Sometimes they let too many animals graze on the land. Other settlers came. They plowed up their grass and planted wheat. The new wheat did not hold the soil as old grass had.

3   Part of the year, the ground was bare. In dry weather, the wind picked up the earth and blew it away. The air was filled with clouds of dust. Neither people nor animals could live in this "dust bowl."

4   We cannot put back the earth that has blown away. But we can try to keep from losing the soil that is still there. New ways of farming are used now. Part of the land is always left with a grass cover. We do not want another dust bowl.

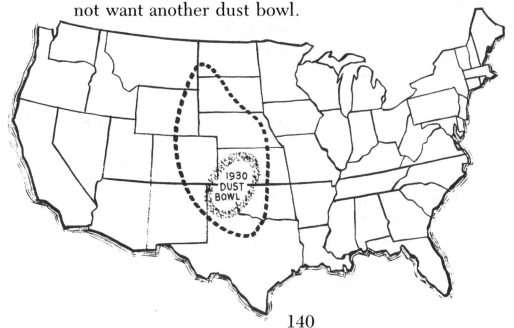

FIND THE ANSWERS

1. The brown snow fell in
   a. New England.   c. the plains.
   b. the West.   d. the South.

2. The word in paragraph 2, sentence 4, that means *to eat grass* is

   _____ .

3. The story says: "In dry weather, the wind picked up the earth and blew *it* away." The word *it* is another word for the

   _____ .

4. The story does not say this, but from what we have read, we can tell that
   a. New England farmers raise a lot of cattle.
   b. wind can carry dust for great distances.
   c. brown snow is better for soil than white snow.

5. What destroyed the land? (Which sentence is exactly like the one in your book?)
   a. Short, thick grass destroyed the plains land.
   b. Brown snow destroyed the land and the cattle.
   c. Wheat and too many cattle had destroyed the land.

6. The main idea of the whole story is that
   a. the wrong use of land can destroy it.
   b. there are dust bowls all over the country.
   c. cattle eat all the wheat in dry weather.

7. The word in sentence 1 that is the opposite of *rose* is

   _____ .

8. Which of the following does this story lead you to believe?
   a. We can always put back soil that has blown away.
   b. Good farms are found in dust bowls in New England.
   c. People did not know they could spoil our resources.

Plant from the Sea

1   Algae are very simple plants. They grow in fresh water or in salt water. Seaweed is algae that grows in salt water. Most seaweed is red or brown in color. The Japanese people use this plant from the sea in many ways. From it, they make a food called *kombu* (kōm bü). Kombu is seaweed that has been dried, cooked, and pressed together. Then it is dried again and cut into long thin pieces. The Japanese eat a lot of kombu and like it very much.

2   Japanese farmers often use seaweed as fertilizer. It makes their plants grow better. Many farmers also find that seaweed makes a fine food for their animals.

3   From seaweed the Japanese also get iodine, which they sell to other countries. Iodine is used in many ways all over the world. It is used in making some medicines. It is added to the salt we use at the table. Scientists even use one form of iodine to "seed" clouds when they want rain to fall.

1. Kombu is a
   a. medicine.   c. food.
   b. drink.   d. toy.

2. The word in the story that means *something used on soil to help plants grow better* is _____ .

3. The story says: "Iodine is used in many ways all over the world. *It* is used in making some medicines." The word *it* takes us back to the word _____ .

4. The story does not say this, but from what we have read, we can tell that
   a. the Japanese use their resources well.
   b. the Japanese only use seaweed as food.
   c. people all over the world eat kombu.

5. How do we use iodine in our food? (Which sentence is exactly like the one in your book?)
   a. We add it to the pepper we take to the table.
   b. It is added to the salt we use at the table.
   c. We put it in the catsup we use at the table.

6. The main idea of the whole story is that
   a. the Japanese eat seaweed when they want rain.
   b. kombu is made into medicine for farmers.
   c. the Japanese use seaweed in many ways.

7. The word in paragraph 1, sentence 7, that is the opposite of *raw* is _____ .

8. Which of the following does this story lead you to believe?
   a. The Japanese feed kombu to their animals.
   b. We could probably learn more about seaweed.
   c. Seaweed is the only useful algae.

Who Has the Salt?

1 All around the world, salt is used on food. Some salt, called rock salt, is mined. There are deep salt mines in the United States. In Michigan, more than a million tons of salt a year come from just one underground mine. But many countries do not have good salt mines. They must find other ways to get salt. They can buy salt from other countries. But if they are near ocean water, they can gather their own salt.

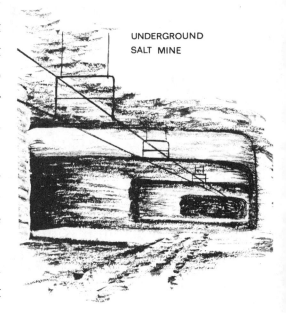

UNDERGROUND SALT MINE

2 In Colombia, a country in South America, the Guajira (gwä hē′rə) Indians take salt from the sea. They make small holes along the beaches. The waves fill the holes with salty water. The sun and wind dry out the water. What is left is pure salt.

3 In the Middle East, salt is taken from the Dead Sea. To help the sun dry out the water faster, a dye is put in the water. This dye helps keep some of the salt from sinking into the ground.

144

1. The Guajira Indians live in
   a. Bolivia.   c. Chile.
   b. Colombia.   d. Brazil.

2. The word in paragraph 3, sentence 2, that means *something used to color other things* is _____.

3. The story says: "But many countries do not have good salt mines. *They* must find other ways to get salt." The word *they* takes us back to the word _____.

4. The story does not say this, but from what we have read, we can tell that
   a. the Guajira do not use salt.
   b. people must have salt.
   c. salt comes from lakes.

5. In the Middle East, what is taken from the Dead Sea? (Which sentence is exactly like the one in your book?)
   a. In the Middle East, salt is taken from the Dead Sea.
   b. In the Middle East, fish are taken from the Dead Sea.
   c. In the Middle East, dye is taken from the Dead Sea.

6. The main idea of the whole story is that
   a. people can take salt from the ocean.
   b. there are salt mines everywhere.
   c. not every country uses salt.

7. The word in paragraph 3, sentence 1, that is the opposite of *given* is _____.

8. Which of the following does the story lead you to believe?
   a. Salt makes holes by sinking into beaches.
   b. Salt tastes better if it is dyed.
   c. People get salt in different ways.

Using Space in Japan

1   Japan is a very beautiful country. But as you know, there is little room for its people to live. This is because mountains cover six out of every seven square miles of Japan.

2   The Japanese understand how to live in their environment. Their living quarters are quite small. Rooms are often separated only by paper screens, yet families live in harmony. There is little land for farming, but wherever there is the smallest amount of open space, something is growing. The Japanese have made an art form out of the miniature garden.

3   Because there is so little land that can be farmed, Japan must buy food from other countries. The Japanese must pay for this food. Therefore, Japan must make goods that it can sell to other countries. It is not surprising that people who have learned to live together in close quarters have also learned to work together. In Japanese factories, people work in teams to build high-quality products. The Japanese are world leaders in making cars and electronic goods such as TVs and computers.

FIND THE ANSWERS

1. Japan must buy food from other
    - a. stores.
    - b. farms.
    - c. countries.
    - d. states.

2. The word in the story that means *very small* is _____.

3. The word *its* in paragraph 1 means _____.

4. The story does not say this, but from what we have read we can tell that
    - a. many Japanese people earn their living by making cars.
    - b. most people in Japan have always been farmers.
    - c. most Japanese people live in big houses outside of the cities.

5. What kinds of products do the Japanese make? (Which sentence is exactly like the one in your book?)
    - a. The Japanese make only electronic goods such as TVs and computers.
    - b. The Japanese are world leaders in making cameras, TVs, VCRs, and computers.
    - c. The Japanese are world leaders in making cars and electronic goods such as TVs and computers.

6. The main idea of the whole story is that
    - a. the Japanese people always feel crowded.
    - b. the Japanese people know how to use space well.
    - c. there are many television sets all over Japan.

7. The word in paragraph 2, sentence 3, that is the opposite of *joined* is _____.

8. Which of the following does the story lead you to believe?
    - a. It is impossible to live in a country with many mountains.
    - b. Space is a resource that should be used wisely.
    - c. Japan has a very small population.

Beehive Houses

1   There are few trees in the Syrian desert. It is hard to get wood. Clay bricks are used for building houses. The desert houses have thick walls. They have only a few small windows to let in light. Holes at the tops of the houses let out smoke.

2   The thick walls keep the houses warm in winter. The high roofs help keep the houses cool in summer. These high round roofs make the houses look like beehives. Strong desert winds blow a lot of dust. The thick walls and few windows protect the people inside from both winds and dust.

3   The beehive houses cost almost nothing to build. They are easy to fix. Houses of this kind have been built for hundreds of years in the Syrian desert. Many desert people would rather live in these houses than in modern buildings.

FIND THE ANSWERS

1. In the Syrian desert, there is not much
   - a. sand.
   - c. wood.
   - b. clay.
   - d. wind.

2. The word in paragraph 3, sentence 1, that means *needed to pay* is _____.

3. The story says: "The beehive houses cost almost nothing to build. *They* are easy to fix." The word *they* takes us back to the word _____.

4. The story does not say this, but from what we have read, we can tell that
   - a. many bees live in the Syrian desert.
   - b. there are many trees in the desert.
   - c. it is dark inside the desert houses.

5. What do the desert winds do? (Which sentence is exactly like the one in your book?)
   - a. The desert winds blow too much rain.
   - b. Strong desert winds blow a lot of dust.
   - c. Desert winds blow a lot of strong bees.

6. The main idea of the whole story is that
   - a. Syrian beehive houses are good desert shelter.
   - b. there is not much wood in the desert.
   - c. desert houses have thin walls and many windows.

7. The word in paragraph 3, sentence 2, that is the opposite of *break* is _____.

8. Which of the following does this article lead you to believe?
   - a. All the people in Syria like to live in beehives.
   - b. Desert people build fires in their houses.
   - c. Many desert people live in very modern buildings.

Houses on Stilts

1   Would you like to live in a house on stilts? In the Philippine Islands in the Pacific Ocean, many farmers build their houses on stilts. The stilts are made from bamboo or wood. The bamboo floor of the house rests on the stilts three to six feet above the ground. A ladder may be used to get in and out of the house. At night for protection, the ladders can be pulled up.

2   When the wind blows, air moves through the space under the house. This helps keep the house cool. There are very heavy rains in the rainy season. Since the floor of a house on stilts is above the ground, it stays dry.

3   In the dry season, farmers make good use of the space under the house. In the heat of the day, cattle and other farm animals rest there. Tools and farm carts can be stored under the house as well.

FIND THE ANSWERS

1. Farmers make good use of the space under the house
   - a. in the dry season.
   - c. in the heat.
   - b. in the wet season.
   - d. in the cold.

2. The word in the story that means *not warm* or *almost cold* is

   _____ .

3. The story says: "Since the floor of a house on stilts is above the ground, *it* stays dry." The word *it* takes us back to the word

   _____ .

4. The story does not say this, but from what we have read, we can tell that
   - a. the space under the houses is never used.
   - b. at night the bamboo ladders cannot be pulled up.
   - c. houses on stilts are good for hot, wet places.

5. How do people get in and out of the house? (Which sentence is exactly like the one in your book?)
   - a. The people use steps to go in and out of the house.
   - b. To go in and out of the house, a ladder is used.
   - c. A ladder may be used to get in and out of the house.

6. The main idea of the whole story is that
   - a. it is easy to build a house on stilts.
   - b. many Philippine houses are built on stilts.
   - c. it is hot and dry in the Philippine Islands.

7. The word in paragraph 2, sentence 3, that is the opposite of *dry*

   is _____ .

8. Which of the following does this story lead you to believe?
   - a. The weather in the Philippines is very warm.
   - b. There are no cows in the Philippines.
   - c. Philippine houses are three-stories high.

Houses the Breezes Blow Through

1   Tahiti is a beautiful island where the weather is never cold and never too hot. There is always a cool breeze off the sea. Here the people do not need houses with thick walls. All they need is shelter from rain and sun.

2   Four posts pounded into the ground form the four corners of a Tahitian (tə hē′shən) house. Poles tied together with bark make the frame of the slanting roof. Palm leaves and other leaves are put over this frame and tied fast. When the roof has a thick cover of leaves, rain runs right off. Mats are made of leaves and grasses. Spread on the ground, they make a floor.

3   Some houses have no walls at all. Others have walls made of palm leaves or bamboo strips. They look like the sides of baskets. Breezes blow through the many small openings in these walls.

4   Roofs and walls made of leaves last only a few years. Then fresh leaves are picked to make new roofs and walls.

1. In Tahiti there is always
     a. very hot weather.   c. cold weather.
     b. a cool breeze.   d. a warm breeze.

2. The word in the story that means *a light wind* is _____.

3. The story says: "Mats are made of leaves and grasses. Spread on the ground, *they* make a floor." The word *they* takes us back to the word _____ .

4. The story does not say this, but from what we have read, we can tell that
     a. Tahitian people do not need shelter.
     b. Tahitians make walls from baskets.
     c. bricks are hard to get in Tahiti.

5. How are mats made? (Which sentence is exactly like the one in your book?)
     a. Mats are made of leaves and grasses.
     b. Mats are made of poles and branches.
     c. Mats are made of palms and thatches.

6. The main idea of the whole story is that
     a. houses on Tahiti are made to suit the weather.
     b. the weather on Tahiti is not very pleasant.
     c. palm trees and bamboo trees grow on the island of Tahiti.

7. The word in paragraph 2, sentence 2, that is the opposite of *apart* is _____ .

8. Which of the following does this story lead you to believe?
     a. Houses in Tahiti cost a lot of money.
     b. Tahitian houses do not take long to build.
     c. Cold weather is a problem in Tahiti.

The Daring People

1   Some small nations are near the sea. The sea became their greatest resource. Some nations, like Holland, sailed the seas to rule over other peoples. Some, like Portugal, crossed the seas to find new land. Still others, like Phoenicia (fə nish′ə), searched the seas looking for new trade routes.

2   Three thousand years ago, the ancient Phoenicians knew more about the sea than any other nation. Phoenicians built the best ships. They were the best navigators.

3   Phoenician sailors sailed far from home. They did this at a time when others were still afraid of the sea and strange places. Phoenicians sailed around Africa. Their ships reached the Far East. They brought back many things. From England, they brought tin. From cities around the Mediterranean Sea, they got such things as silver and linen. The Phoenicians traded what they found to other countries.

4   From 1000 B.C. to 800 B.C. little Phoenicia was very important in the ancient world. Because its people were daring, Phoenicia became a great nation of sailors and traders.

1. The ancient Phoenicians were the best
   a. farmers.
   c. fighters.
   b. navigators.
   d. rulers.

2. The word in the story that means *groups of people living together in one country under the same government* is _____ .

3. The story says: "Phoenicians built the best ships. *They* were the best navigators." The word *they* takes us back to the word

   _____ .

4. The story does not say this, but from what we have read, we can tell that
   a. the Phoenicians kept all the things they found.
   b. Phoenicians exchanged ideas as well as products.
   c. most ancient people were not afraid of the sea.

5. What did the Phoenicians get from England? (Which sentence is exactly like the one in your book?)
   a. From England, they brought linen.
   b. They brought people from England.
   c. From England, they brought tin.

6. The main idea of the whole story is that
   a. the ancient Phoenicians were great sailors and traders.
   b. little countries were not important in ancient times.
   c. all the ancient nations had sailors to explore the world.

7. The word in paragraph 4, sentence 1, that is the opposite of *modern* is _____ .

8. Which of the following does this story lead you to believe?
   a. The Phoenicians and the Dutch are much alike.
   b. Phoenicians are the best sailors who ever lived.
   c. Tin was once mined in England.

The Passing of the Old Ships

1   Today there are many ways for passengers and cargo to travel. But once, if you had to go to a country across the ocean or send a cargo over the seas, you had only one choice: the sailing ship.

2   By 1900 steamships were on the seas. But some sailing ships were used until the mid-1900s. By then, the old ships could be bought cheaply. They were still good for the long trade between England and Australia and along the coasts. Good crews made this possible.

3   One of the last of the sailing cargo ships was a bark called the *Passat*. Unlike the older ships, this one had a body, or hull, made of steel instead of wood. It was a strong ship with an engine and four masts. One thing we know about the *Passat* is that a woman, Anne Stanley Moss, was a crew member on one of its last voyages.

4   Steamships took over more and more. Soon it was hard to find sailors who knew how to handle the old sailing ships. Sailing without experienced crews was dangerous. By the 1950s, the good old ships no longer sailed for business.

1. Sailing ships need
      a. steel hulls.   c. experienced crews.
      b. good engines.   d. five masts.

2. The word in the story that means *goods carried by ships* is

   _____ .

3. The story says: ". . . the old ships could be bought cheaply. They

   were still good. . . ." The word *they* means _____ .

4. The story does not say this, but from what we have read, we can
   tell that
      a. Sailors never liked the old sailing ships.
      b. Some people tried hard to keep sailing ships going.
      c. There were always many ways to travel over seas.

5. What kept the old ships useful for the long trade between England
   and Australia? (Which sentence is exactly like the one in your
   book?)
      a. Good crews made this possible.
      b. A new steel hull made better ships.
      c. It was easy to find good sailors.

6. The main idea of the whole story is that
      a. Today, no one can sail a ship.
      b. Steamships took over the business of the sailing ships.
      c. There have been very few changes in the way people travel
         on the sea.

7. The word in paragraph 4, sentence 3, that is the opposite of *un-

   trained* is _____ .

8. Which of the following does this story lead you to believe?
      a. All women love to sail.
      b. It is easy to sail a big ship.
      c. Today, people only sail for fun.

A Ship Called the Flyboat

1   Holland is a tiny country. It is no more than 200 miles long and just over 150 miles wide. Yet in the 1600s, this small nation in the North Sea was a great sea power. Her more than 10,000 ships went to all parts of the world.

2   In the 1600s, the Dutch made a ship called a flyboat. It was a slow, clumsy boat, but it could carry a lot of cargo. Since the Dutch could carry more cargo, they could do more trading. Trading brought about the building of new colonies.

3   It was not long before there were Dutch colonies in the Americas, in Africa, in the West Indies, and in the East Indies. The great city of New York began as the Dutch colony New Amsterdam.

4   The Dutch used the seas to become a great trading nation. They also used the seas to become a great power in the world. Dutch ships helped Holland rule other lands for more than 200 years.

1. The Dutch made a ship called a
    a. flyboat.   c. seaboat.
    b. sailboat.   d. bugboat.

2. The word in the story that means *not graceful* or *awkward* is

    _____ .

3. The word *they* in paragraph 2 means the _____ .

4. The story does not say this, but from what we have read, we can
    tell that
    a. the Dutch flyboat is a small, fast sailing ship.
    b. a country need not be large to be powerful.
    c. New Amsterdam is a colony in New Jersey.

5. When did the Dutch make the flyboat? (Which sentence is
    exactly like the one in your book?)
    a. In the 1600s, the Dutch made a ship called a flyboat.
    b. In 1692, the Dutch made a ship called the sailboat.
    c. In the 1700s, the Dutch made a ship called the flatboat.

6. The main idea of the whole story is that
    a. flyboats were often 200 miles long and 150 miles wide.
    b. all the Dutch people left Holland in large flyboats.
    c. Holland used the seas to become a powerful country.

7. The word in paragraph 1, sentence 1, that is the opposite of *big*

    is _____ .

8. Which of the following does this story lead you to believe?
    a. Flyboats made Holland a great flying nation.
    b. People who master the sea can build great nations.
    c. The Dutch people did not like to trade in Africa.

Building on Ideas

1   The ancient Romans built a great empire and ruled almost the entire world they knew. They did this without coming up with many new ideas or inventions. The Romans did, however, find new ways to use what they learned from the nations they conquered.

2   Take the arch, for example. The shape of the arch makes it strong. With arches, it is possible to load a great deal of weight above an open space. The ancient Egyptians, Babylonians, and Greeks all used arches before the Romans did. They used them mainly to build underground drains.

3   The Romans used arches in many kinds of structures. One important use was aqueducts, which they built to carry water from country lakes to cities and towns. The Romans built the aqueducts high above ground. Gravity moved the water down the duct. Then the water went through pipes. It flowed into taps that are not so different from the ones we have today.

4   Bringing water from far away made life better in Roman towns and cities. The aqueducts were so well made that parts of them still exist today.

FIND THE ANSWERS

1. The ancient Egyptians, Babylonians, and Greeks knew how to build
   a. aqueducts.   c. castles.
   b. arches.   d. engineers.
2. The word in the story that means *very old* is _____.
3. The word *they* in paragraph 3 means _____.
4. The story does not say this, but from what we have read, we can tell that
   a. the Romans must have had great armies.
   b. daily life in ancient Rome was not so different from our life today.
   c. most Romans lived in cities and towns.
5. Why is the arch useful in buildings? (Which sentence is exactly like the one in your book?)
   a. The shape of the arch makes it strong.
   b. The shape of the arch is beautiful.
   c. The arch is easy to make.
6. The main idea of the whole story is that
   a. the ancient Romans built a mighty empire.
   b. thanks to the aqueducts ancient Romans had running water in their homes.
   c. the ancient Romans made good use of earlier ideas and inventions.
7. The word in paragraph 3, sentence 3, that is the opposite of *torn down* is _____.
8. Which of the following does the story lead you to believe?
   a. The ancient Romans were more intelligent than the ancient Greeks.
   b. The ancient Romans were interested in practical things.
   c. The ancient Romans never invented anything themselves.

More Than Nothing

1   Very early people kept track of "how many" by using small objects. For example, they might have lined up five pebbles to stand for five baskets of grain. Later on, they made tally marks like these: ||||, which means 5 things.

2   In time people began to use words and symbols instead of marks. These number systems were fine for counting. However, people had a hard time doing arithmetic problems with them.

3   When communities become more complicated, arithmetic became very important. People needed to solve number problems so they could trade with each other and construct roads and buildings.

4   People in both India and Central America came up with the same idea: zero. Their new idea made doing math problems easier. The symbol for zero could be used to mark "empty" places. Think of the number one hundred and seven. How could you write it in figures without a zero? The zero tells you the tens place is empty.

5   Without the zero, we would not have science and math as we know it today. Most advances in technology would be impossible.

FIND THE ANSWERS

1. It is hard to solve number problems without
   a. words.
   c. pebbles.
   b. zero.
   d. technology.

2. The word in the story that means *find the answer to* is

   _____.

3. The word *they* in paragraph 3 means _____.

4. The story does not say this, but from what we have read we can tell that
   a. very early people did not build roads.
   b. you cannot solve problems without a zero.
   c. people never use tally marks anymore.

5. What were the early number systems good for? (Which sentence is exactly like the one in your book?)
   a. These systems were needed to build roads.
   b. These systems were used to hold "empty" places.
   c. These number systems were fine for counting.

6. The main idea of the story is that
   a. early people were not as intelligent as we are today.
   b. over time people changed their number systems to meet their changing needs.
   c. without the idea of zero we would not have TVs or computers.

7. The word in paragraph 3, sentence 1, that is the opposite of *simple* is _____.

8. Which of the following does the story lead you to believe?
   a. We do arithmetic differently from the way early people did.
   b. Before people came up with the idea of zero, they couldn't add or subtract numbers.
   c. Indians and Central Americans both used "0" for zero.

New Designs for Space

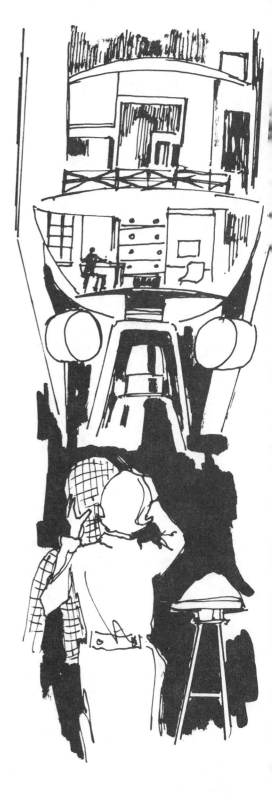

1   In the 1940s the first rocket plane, the X-1, was about to be tested. The pilot would have to fly at great pressures and still breathe comfortably. Scientists called in a sculptor, Alice Chatham.

2   She began to work on designs for special rubber masks that would fit tightly over the nose and the mouth of the pilot. They had to be airtight so the pilot could breathe extra oxygen when flying at high altitudes.

3   The designer carefully made the model mask by hand. When the pilot tested her special design, he flew the plane faster than the speed of sound and the design worked!

4   After that, Alice Chatham also designed and tested suits and helmets for pilots flying faster than the speed of sound. She even made a dummy exactly like an Air Force major. It helped her test the way the suits would work.

5   New research will make space stations where humans will not have to wear spacesuits. They will live in the space stations and breathe air that is brought from earth. They will study even better ways to live in space.

1. The first test pilots needed
   a. a small rocket.
   c. special rubber masks.
   b. a dummy.
   d. a space station.

2. The word in the story that means *a gas without color or smell that is part of the air we breathe* is _____ .

3. The word *she* in paragraph 4 takes us back to the name

   _____ .

4. The story does not say this, but from what we have read, we can tell that
   a. the people inside a laboratory will find it hard to breathe.
   b. weather can be studied only inside some space stations.
   c. spacesuits have to be tested carefully.

5. What will people do in space stations? (Which sentence is exactly like the one in your book?)
   a. They will make more spacesuits.
   b. They will study even better ways to live in space.
   c. They will study new designs for breathing.

6. The main idea of the whole story is that
   a. spacesuits are very comfortable to wear.
   b. the people breathe only extra air.
   c. past research will help future space study.

7. The word in paragraph 1, sentence 2, that is the opposite of *uncomfortably* is _____ .

8. Which of the following does this story lead you to believe?
   a. New ways to live in space are possible.
   b. People do not need oxygen.
   c. Earth does not have enough tests.

The Wonderful Hammer

In very old stories told in Norway, Thor was the god of thunder and lightning. Thunder came from the rumbling of the wheels of his chariot. Lightning came from the sparks that flew when he threw his hammer. Thor's hammer was a magic weapon that always struck its mark and then returned to Thor's hand. It could become large and heavy, or it could become very small.

Thor did not always have this wonderful hammer. He got it because Loki, the god of mischief, made a bet with a dwarf! This was the way it began.

Loki saw Thor's beautiful wife asleep under a tree with her long yellow hair spread out around her. For a joke, Loki cut off all her hair. Thor's wife cried and cried when she woke and found her hair gone! Thor was very angry, and so were the other gods who were Thor's friends.

"Don't punish me!" Loki cried when the gods caught him. "Let me go, and I will replace the hair. I will get hair of pure gold for her that will grow like her own."

The gods let Loki go. Loki hurried to the dwarfs who lived deep under the earth. The dwarfs were very clever at working with metals. Before long they had spun hair of pure yellow gold for Loki. The dwarfs also made two gifts for Loki to give to Thor's friends. One was a spear that would always find its mark. The other was a ship that would always find fair winds and sail quickly. Loki was very pleased. The gods would forgive him when they saw these wonderful things.

167

On his way home, Loki met another dwarf whose name was Brock. Loki showed Brock his magic gifts.

"Your brother Sindri is clever at making things," Loki said. "But I'll bet my head Sindri can't make things as fine as these."

"I'll take that bet," Brock said. "Let us go to Sindri's workshop."

First Sindri made a golden pig. It could not only travel quickly over land and sea with a rider on its back! It also gave off light at night! Next Sindri made a golden ring. Every ninth day, this ring would make eight more rings just like it! Last of all, Sindri made the hammer.

Loki and Brock traveled together to the home of the gods. Loki gave his gifts to the gods first. The beautiful golden hair went to Thor's wife. Odin, Thor's friend and the most powerful of the gods, got the magic spear. Loki gave the magic ship to Freya, the goddess of beauty.

Now it was Brock's turn. He gave the magic golden

ring to Odin. The magic golden pig went to Freya. Thor got the hammer.

After looking at all the gifts, the gods decided Brock's gifts were much finer than Loki's, and that the hammer was best of all.

"You bet your head," Brock said to Loki. "Now I have won it, and I will cut it off!"

Loki had to think fast.

"You may have my head then," cried Loki. "But don't touch my neck. I didn't bet my neck!"

Brock grumbled, but he couldn't collect his bet.

And that is how, because of Loki, the god of thunder and lightning got his wonderful hammer.

549 words

Fill in your record chart after each test. Beside the page numbers, put a one for each correct question. Put zero in the box of each question you missed. At the far right, put your total. Eight is a perfect score for each test.

When you finish all the tests in a concept, total your scores by question. The highest possible score for each question in one concept is the number of stories.

When you have taken several tests, check to see which questions you get right each time. Which ones are you missing? Find the places where you need help. For example, if you are missing Question 3 often, ask for help in learning to use directing words.

As you begin each concept, copy the chart onto lined paper. Down the left side are the test page numbers. Across the top are the question numbers and the kinds of questions. For example, each Question 1 in this book asks you to recall a fact. Your scores for each question show how well you are learning each skill.

Your Reading Scores — Concept I

Question	1 fact	2 vocabulary	3 antecedent	4 inference	5 confirming content	6 main idea	7 vocabulary opposites	8 inference	Total for Page
Page 15									
17									
19									
21									
23									
25									
27									
29									
31									
33									
35									
37									
39									
41									
43									
45									
47									
49									
51									
53									
55									
57									
59									
61									
Totals by question									

Your Reading Scores

Concept III

Question Page	fact 1	vocabulary 2	antecedent 3	inference 4	confirming content 5	main idea 6	vocabulary opposites 7	inference 8	Total for Page
Page 119									
121									
123									
125									
127									
129									
131									
133									
135									
137									
139									
141									
143									
145									
147									
149									
151									
153									
155									
157									
159									
161									
163									
165									
Totals by question									

Your Reading Scores

Concept II

Question Page	fact 1	vocabulary 2	antecedent 3	inference 4	confirming content 5	main idea 6	vocabulary opposites 7	inference 8	Total for Page
Page 67									
69									
71									
73									
75									
77									
79									
81									
83									
85									
87									
89									
91									
93									
95									
97									
99									
101									
103									
105									
107									
109									
111									
113									
Totals by question									

171